# Golden Eggs

# Golden Eggs

## Spiritual Wisdom for Birthing Our Lives

GAY LYNN WILLIAMSON

AND

DAVID WILLIAMSON, D. MIN.

Health Communications, Inc.
Deerfield Beach, Florida

**Library of Congress Cataloging-in-Publication Data**

Williamson, Gay, (date)
    Golden eggs : spiritual wisdom for birthing our lives / Gay Lynn
Williamson and David Williamson.
       p.   cm.
    ISBN 1-55874-416-9 (trade paper)
    1. Spiritual life. 2. Interviews. 3. Unity School of Christianity.
I. Williamson, David, (date) II. Title.
    BL624W56 1996
    291.4—dc20

                                            96-30192
                                            CIP

©1996 Gay Lynn Williamson and David Williamson
ISBN 1-55874-416-9

Publisher: Health Communications, Inc.
         3201 S.W. 15th Street
         Deerfield Beach, Florida 33442-8190

*Cover design by José Villavicencio*

*To Myrtle and Charles Fillmore,*
*wife and husband, who together*
*birthed the Unity movement as their*
*golden contribution*
*to humanity.*

Within you
is unborn possibility
of limitless living,
and yours is the
privilege of giving
birth to it.

# Contents

# Acknowledgments

Our gratitude to our publishers, Peter Vegso and Gary Seidler, for their encouragement of our leading-edge explorations. Many thanks to our editors Barbara Whelehan, Christine Belleris, Matthew Diener for their guidance and refining touches.

We appreciate the many authors who inspired us with their books and articles on the power of the Divine Feminine and Masculine in every person. We wish we could have interviewed many more people and included many additional voices in this book. As we would see or hear someone giving birth to a creative and transformative endeavor in our world, we would exclaim, "Oh, that would be a great person to talk with!" We did talk with more people than we could include here, so we trust every one will understand.

Our sincere thanks to Unity School, Unity centers and conferences across the country who invited us to speak. Also, Religious Science and the Association of Transpersonal Psychology warmly welcomed us as speakers. Our travels afforded us the opportunity to meet and interview the

contributors in *Golden Eggs*. We wrote and compiled this
book while traveling in our 24-foot trailer across America.

Finally, we feel a special mystical connection to the figure
of the Black Madonna. We encountered her again and again
in outer and inner ways, confirming that there is a womb of
the world where all is born out of sacred darkness.

**Our Lady of Guadalupe**
**One of a number of Black Madonnas**

# 1

# Spiritual Wisdom for Birthing Our Lives

## The Goose That Laid the Golden Eggs

There once was a lucky man
Who lived in days of old.
The gods had blessed him with a goose
Whose eggs were purest gold.
And day by day she laid these eggs
And honked her proud delight.
And day by day these goose eggs shone
With glowing golden light.
And yet this greedy man,
Who watched his fortune grow,
Grew restless with his golden goose
And felt her much too slow.
"You silly goose!" The man complained.
"You must obey your master.
Your golden eggs are welcome here,
But you must lay them faster!"
The goose was glad to try her best,
And eager to obey,
So still she laid her golden eggs—

But only one a day.
At last the foolish man declared
That he could wait no more.
He slew the goose and cut her up
To find the golden store.
He slew the goose to find the gold;
He searched the goose with care.
But to this greedy man's dismay,
He found no treasure there.
The goose was dead, the goose was gone,
The goose was growing cold.
No more this magic goose would lay
Her eggs of gleaming gold.

Alas, this silly, grasping man
The gods had blessed before,
Now lost the plenty that he had
In greed for having more.

AESOP'S FABLES
—*RETOLD IN VERSE BY TOM PAXTON*

# The Goose and Her Golden Eggs

The fable of the goose that lays golden eggs speaks of a wondrous creature who has the ability to give birth to treasures as a natural expression of itself. Sadly, the story usually emphasizes the greedy, foolish farmer who kills the goose to get all the golden eggs at once. Caring for the goose and keeping it in good health so it can continue to bear its treasure certainly would have averted disaster. However, we want to explore the wonderful nature of the goose that bears these golden eggs. The goose, of course, is you and me. We have the innate ability to birth treasures from within ourselves. The good we long for and seek is already within us!

Human beings have written, talked, and sung about gold as a symbol of all that is precious and valuable in life. Yet the metal remains elusive, buried in the ground somewhere, requiring miners to dig it out. That requirement doesn't apply when considering the treasures of ourselves. The rich lode we can discover is not

> **The eggs are the treasures that help us understand our natural abilities, not only because eggs come from within, but also because eggs have a life within themselves.**

buried somewhere but already an integral part of us. We can birth it! "The Kingdom [abundance, talent, wisdom, riches, love, health, joy] of God is within." (Luke 17:21 NIV) We need not look in another place or time, but within ourselves, here and now.

The eggs are the treasures that help us understand our natural abilities, not only because eggs come from within, but also because eggs have a life within themselves. That life hatches forth into a whole new expression that is more than we could have made. The seed principle is at work here. Remember the old saying, "You can count the seeds in an apple, but who can count the apples in a seed?" We bring forth the new expression, and that new life impacts others and our world in countless ways.

A dream revealed to Gay Lynn the cover of the book when we began collecting and compiling the text. On the cover was a golden egg. In the golden egg there appeared something alive and growing. We accepted the image as a sign and began to call the book *Golden Eggs.* We researched the symbol of the egg and found that it was used by the Hindu Vedas and Plato, and represented the "cosmic birth-giver." As the cosmic birth-giver it also personifies the omnipresent mother; being omnipresent, she is like the air. In Hebrew, spirit means breath and is a feminine term. From Latin, spirit derives from spiritus, which means "to breathe or blow." We see the world-mother as the *anima-mundi,* everywhere present as the Great Spirit, and elegantly represented by the egg. In the egg, or embryo, our life journey originates. The egg also symbolizes the resurrection in Christianity, which may explain the centuries-old custom of coloring eggs at Easter.

We are the goose that lays the golden eggs, as Aesop's classic fable reveals. We have golden egg-making wonders within us. This is manifested by countless human creations—companies, art works, inventions, books, churches, schools,

plays, governments, farms, relationships, families, sports—
to name a few.

What is our birthing ability all about? How do we do give
birth to creations of value and progress? How do we combine
the powers of our Divine Feminine and Divine Masculine
energies to conceive these golden eggs within ourselves? How
do we nurture them in gestation, go through the birthing
process, and make our own unique contributions to the world?

Everyone has a creative, Divine Feminine potency that is
being rediscovered, reclaimed and embraced by both women
and men as they tap into that innate womb of the world that
many ancients honored.

We present some great stories, images, parables, fables,
and examples in *Golden Eggs*. We talk with Charles Garfield,
Barbara Marx Hubbard, James Redfield, Jerry Jampolsky,
Angeles Arrien, O.C. and Robbie Smith, Walter Starcke, Pat
and Jack Barker, Carol Lynn
Pearson, Patricia Sun, Steven
Halpern, Rinaldo Brutoco,
and others who have given
birth and share their stories
of personal and global transformation. However, our goal
is to empower you to understand your creative genesis

> **The Golden Egg is
> the metaphor of your
> wholeness, reminding
> you that within you
> is the embryonic energy
> of the cosmos, creatively
> birthing your daily life.**

and conceive the fulfilling offspring that only you can birth.

The Golden Egg is the metaphor of your wholeness,
reminding you that within you is the embryonic energy of the
cosmos, creatively birthing your daily life. How conscious are
you of the birthing process? In your career, relationships,
spiritual development and world, how do you enter the
birthing chamber in yourself? How do the dynamic and

magnetic energies of the masculine and feminine within you unite to give birth?

Aesop's fable of "The Goose That Laid the Golden Eggs" provides insights in honoring the goose as well as the wisdom to birth your own gold each day. We read the fable to leading-edge people in the consciousness movement, and they have shared how this fable can help you understand the birthing process going on in your life.

As we approach the eve of the 21st century, we are seeing the crisis of the planet; yet it is the crisis of *birth*, not death, as some might think. Birth is powerful, messy, noisy—not always neat and pretty. We are experiencing the struggle and birth pains of labor as a global community birthing itself right now. For instance, our businesses and corporations are undergoing massive change and turmoil, many of them searching for a new model which honors people and the planet as well as making a profit.

> **As we approach the eve of the 21st century, we are seeing the crisis of the planet; yet it is the crisis of *birth*, not death, as some might think. Birth is powerful, messy, noisy—not always neat and pretty.**

Because our Western culture is the only one to separate the masculine and feminine into two distinct characteristics, how do we begin to use new language that includes the marriage of these and creatively synthesize them into our daily life personally and in our cultural consciousness?

Let the words and images evoked on these pages be the midwife to your own divine birth.

# In Search of the Soul

A few years ago, the word soul was practically never used by psychologists and psychiatrists. Perhaps only in the sanctity of churches was there reference to "man's immortal soul." Now soul is one of the most popular terms in contemporary society, and it has assumed more prominence. Books such as *Chicken Soup for the Soul*™ and *Care of the Soul* have become bestsellers. It has even penetrated the secular, corporate world: A large conference on "Transforming the Soul of Business" was recently held at Hilton Head, South Carolina.

Soul is most often thought of as an eternal entity embodied within us. William Blake frequently referred to the body as the portion of the soul that is discerned by the five senses. The soul is the eternal part of us that lives and interacts through the body. So we are soul embodied in flesh, and we are flesh imbued with soul. We are a spark of Divinity.

In the time of St. Augustine, the question of whether women even had a soul was debated. At that time it was quite doubtful. And yet today no one questions that each of us has an organic, living, energetic part of us that we call soul.

Noted Swiss psychologist Dr. Carl Jung asked his patients to draw mandalas, which in Sanskrit means "circles." Found in Oriental art, mandalas are symbols of the universe. Dr. Jung looked for representations of the soul through these artistic expressions. He became aware that we have a center to our personality, a core within the psyche, which in Greek means "soul." This soul center is an energy source within itself to which everything is related. He noted, "The energy of the central point is manifested in the almost irresistible compulsion and urge to 'become what one is,' just as every organism is driven to assume the form that is characteristic of its nature, no matter what the circumstances. This center is not felt or thought of as the ego but, if one may so express it, as the 'self.' Although the center is represented by an innermost point, it is surrounded by a periphery containing everything that belongs to the self—the paired opposites that make up the total personality."

The golden egg is a mandala of the soul. The periphery, or eggshell, contains everything that belongs to you. Within the egg lie all the different components of consciousness and unconsciousness, and various levels of awareness. The egg serves as a simple representation of the inner life, but on deeper examination you discover its complexity.

You are multifaceted and have many parts to your soul. An East Indian expression refers to it as a "conglomerate soul." The golden egg has become for us a symbol of the journey of the self, relating to the birthing of the soul and enhancing spiritual understanding. The egg appeared regularly in many of the mandala drawings of Dr. Jung's patients. You, too, are holding the golden eggs of possibility within you, and are on the journey to realizing your true self and being the person you were meant to be.

In *Intimations of Immortality,* William Wordsworth speaks of our soul birth in this way:

> Our birth is but a sleep and a forgetting:
> The Soul that rises with us, our life's Star,

Hath had elsewhere its setting,
And cometh from afar:
Not in entire forgetfulness,
And not in utter nakedness,
But trailing clouds of glory do we come
From God, who is our home. . . .

Saint Teresa of Avila said, "The soul is capable of much more than we can image. It is very important for any soul that practices prayer . . . not to hold itself back and stay in one corner. Let it walk through those dwelling places which are up above, down below, and to the sides, since God has given it such great dignity." So expand your exploration to look for your soul experience in every corner of your life, not just on occasion but every day, everywhere.

Where are you on the journey to soul discovery? How do you care for and nourish your soul? What are you looking forward to today that will help you get in tune with your soul? In truth the soul is the most creative, energizing aspect of your life. In your relationship with yourself, you touch the most generative part of your being through the soul.

Are you paying attention to the signs and signals? Do you

> **In your relationship with yourself, you touch the most generative part of your being through the soul. Are you paying attention to the signs and signals? Do you feel the awe of spirit reflected in yourself and in all living creatures? You are awesome, yet in your hurry/worry day you may give little or no attention to the center of your life.**

feel the awe of spirit reflected in yourself and in all living creatures? You are awesome, yet in your hurry/worry day you may
give little or no attention to the center of your life. Carl Jung
once said that we need to give attention to the daily needs of
our soul. He put the emphasis on the *daily need,* because we
often pay our soul, the core of our being, little or no attention.

We search for the wisdom of the soul, and long to be wisely
attuned to our soul-wisdom. And what is wisdom? The Apocrypha in the Wisdom literature describes her great beauty:

Within her is a spirit intelligent, holy,
unique, manifold, subtle,
active, incisive, unsullied,
lucid, invulnerable, benevolent, sharp,
irresistible, beneficent, loving to humankind,
steadfast, dependable, unperturbed,
almighty, all-surveying,
penetrating all intelligent, pure
and most subtle spirits;
for Wisdom is quicker to move than any motion;
she is so pure, she pervades and permeates all things.
She is a breath of the power of God,
pure emanation of the glory of the Almighty;
hence nothing impure can find a way into her.
She is a reflection of the eternal light,
untarnished mirror of God's active power,
image of God's goodness.

THE WISDOM OF SOLOMON *7:22-26*
*FROM THE* APOCRYPHA, JERUSALEM BIBLE

The Greek word for wisdom is "Sophia." Early in Jesus' ministry, he was called Sophia, "Teacher of Wisdom." We want to set Sophia free, to birth Wisdom, and invite her into an intimate partnership with us as a trusted friend, a sister to our soul. Traveling into the inner realms of ourselves, our soul-sister Sophia is a loving presence always ready to illuminate our way through our fears, doubts, and struggles. For it is often in our darkness where her companionship is felt most intensely.

When the church fathers were deciding what Greek word they would use to represent the Christ Spirit to the early church, they had to choose between Logos, the male image, and Sophia, the female image. Logos won out. Logos, we might say, was the head, Sophia was the heart. Imagine how differently the Gospel of John might be if it began like this: "In the beginning was Sophia and Sophia was God. She was in the beginning with God. All things came into being through her, and without her not one thing came into being."

> **Imagine how differently the Gospel of John might be if it began like this:** *"In the beginning was Sophia and Sophia was God. She was in the beginning with God. All things came into being through her, and without her not one thing came into being."*

What has come into being in her was life, and the life was the light of all people. The light shines in the darkness, and the darkness did not overcome it." (John 1:1-5)

It sure makes a lot more sense to have Sophia and God in the Divine Partnership bringing forth the life. We can relate to that partnership since it is in tune with the way we live—in companionship, consort and union.

> **"And Sophia became flesh and lived among us, and we have seen her glory . . . full of grace and truth."**
> **(John 1:14)**

"And Sophia became flesh and lived among us, and we have seen her glory . . . full of grace and truth." (John 1:14)

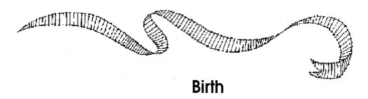

## Birth

Let me express myself in even a clearer way.
The fruitful person
gives birth
out of the very same foundation
from which the creator begets the eternal Word
or Creative Energy
and it is from this core
that one becomes fruitfully pregnant.
And in this power of birthing
God is as fully verdant
and as wholly flourishing in full joy
and in all honor
as he/she is in him/herself.
The divine rapture
is unimaginably great.
It is ineffable.

MEDITATIONS WITH MEISTER ECKHART
BY MATTHEW FOX
FROM THE TEACHINGS OF MEISTER ECKHART

# 2

# Dawning of a New Consciousness

# Thoughts from David:

## Dawning of a New Consciousness

Two words that have become popular and widely used today, especially in labeling and marketing many products, are "organic" and "natural."

I grew up with these terms in the 1940s and '50s. My parents were both chiropractors with a busy practice called the Natural Health Clinic in Detroit. I was exposed to a wide range of natural foods and health therapies, most of which I rebelled against, especially as a teenager. However, I read copies of *Prevention* before it became the popular journal it is today. I read my mother's articles in well-known health magazines found in health-food stores and doctors' waiting rooms. I planted vegetable scraps from the family kitchen in the garden and composted all the leaves every fall. Later, I came to respect what I had ridiculed or felt burdened by as a child and teen.

I founded a holistic and wellness center in my large ministry in Detroit and wrote my doctoral dissertation on this work I called "The Health Church." I extended the wellness work beyond special programs to minister more totally to the whole person.

I came to realize that it is not just a matter of eating more organically grown foods and living more naturally, as important as that is. *We,* ourselves, are organic and the Earth is a living organism herself. Our souls are organic, fertile, dynamic, creative. All these words refer to change and growth. "Life is a progress," said Emerson. You are in process—not static, fixed, solid, set, rigid, secure. You are evolving. You can't stick your foot into the same stream twice, as Heraclitus said. And you can't stick the same foot into the same stream, because your foot is constantly changing at the cellular level.

> **Our souls are organic, fertile, dynamic, creative. All these words refer to change and growth.**

You need to re-examine everyday ways of imaging and talking about your life. You may think and speak of a Newtonian world of solid things that can be counted and always relied upon to be what it looks like, rather than an Einsteinian conception of quantum physics that is energetic, fluid, dynamic, and probably isn't what it looks like.

Take this thinking and apply it to your daily life. In the old concept of interaction you saw yourself as separate. You saw yourself as a body separate from other bodies. Inside yourself you may have felt separate from your thoughts, your feelings, from other people, and from all other living things. You may have erroneously adopted the old Newtonian model and applied it to your life. You are beginning to understand the dynamics of the holographic universe and the holographic brain, and you see now that there is an underlying unity. We are all connected energetically and dynamically through fields of radiant waves and particles of energy. Your thoughts and feelings are intimately interactive in this cosmic soup. You understand now that your thoughts and feelings have a direct impact on your body and the field of energy around you. You may have come to delight in this awareness through the enormously popular bestselling book called *The Celestine Prophecy* by James Redfield. In this fictional story, the characters begin to see their auras and how their feelings and thoughts can energize or dissipate the energy fields around themselves and others.

Whether you can see the auras or not, you can sense your energy draining when you are with someone who is sucking the life energy from everyone in their vicinity. You can also experience the vibrancy when you are with someone who is joyful and sharing their energy with others. Your soul is organic and senses and reads the vibrational tones just as naturally as you see with your eyes or hear with your ears. You sense or intuit with the organic soul.

Watch for the meaningful happenings and coincidences in your life, and act on them.

> **Whether you can see the auras or not, you can sense your energy draining when you are with someone who is sucking the life energy from everyone in their vicinity. You can also experience the vibrancy when you are with someone who is joyful and sharing their energy with others. Your soul is organic and senses and reads the vibrational tones just as naturally as you see with your eyes or hear with your ears. You sense or intuit with the organic soul.**

When you begin to open yourself to the mystical experiences, your life is like the receptive womb. In order to become impregnated, the womb must be receptive for the gift of incarnation to be conceived. Ask yourself, "How receptive am I?"

James Redfield was receptive to the adventure story that was birthed through him, and there were many challenges and seeming roadblocks along the way. He decided to self-publish the first edition after commercial publishers rejected his work. The book eventually topped *The New York Times* bestseller list for months. It is hard to imagine, but he could have let this golden egg go unhatched.

Jesus told a parable about sowing seeds. The seed that fell on receptive ground blossomed into life. You receive the seeds or golden eggs of wisdom, but unless you plant and cultivate them in the receptive, organic matrix of your soul life, they will not bring forth new life or creation.

We are giving birth to our Divinity. On a planetary level, we are going through what Teilhard de Chardin called "cosmo-genesis." We are experiencing regeneration of our physical bodies, the body-politic, and our body of knowledge.

The regenerating of the male and female relationship may be one of the most challenging transformations in our society today as women awaken to their strength and men become aware of their gentleness. As individuals, each of us more fully embraces our inner feminine and masculine.

Let us become conscious and reformation-minded as we confront the thousands of ways we oppress rather than liberate our Divine potential. Barbara Marx Hubbard calls the process "co-creative coupling." We are co-creative equals together.

Receiving is an integral part of your ability to conceive anything. Are you a good receiver? Most would automatically say, "Well, of course, I'm a great receiver!" But check this out the next time someone pays you a compliment. Do you really receive it? Or do you say, "Well, that was nothing. I didn't do that much. No big deal." You may find that it is much easier in some ways to believe the not-so-good stuff about yourself. When it comes to receiving the praise and appreciation of others you may feel awkward and uncomfortable.

> **Receiving is an integral part of your ability to conceive anything. Are you a good receiver?**

Try it with your friends some time. Take turns and listen to absolutely positive comments of who you are and how you have touched people's lives. It can be hard to just breathe and accept these affirmations, and yet at your core level you need to *receive* and honor the good things about yourself and one another. It is the first stage of being open to Spirit having a relationship with your soul, through your relationships with one another, as Redfield so clearly describes in his adventure story, and as Hubbard so beautifully exemplifies in her life.

Opportunity
is God
synchronistically
tapping at the door
of our soul.

# The Celestine Soul:
# A Conversation with James Redfield

*The Celestine Prophecy* came to Redfield as an adventure novel. The reader is drawn into a search, set in the forests of Peru, for an ancient manuscript that contains nine key insights that the human race is predicted to embrace as it moves toward a completely spiritual culture on Earth.

Spreading almost entirely by word of mouth, the book has gained a phenomenal readership since it was introduced in Unity churches, spiritual networks, and metaphysical bookstores a couple of years ago. James met with us at the Association of Unity Churches People's Convention in Alexandria, Virginia.

**David:** Your book, which has been given the new classification "Transformative Fiction" by the publishing field, has become a number-one bestseller. Why has the book found such a huge audience?

**James:** There are so many people right now searching for spiritual fulfillment. For at least the last 25 years, we have been asking, "Isn't there something more?" Now we're saying: "Wait a minute! There's something more, something more than just the religious dogma that I've been exposed to. There's some clearer understanding of what life is all about."

**James Redfield and David Williamson**

So I think we're searching. And it's not just my book, it's many other books. It's the historical position that we're in. We're ready to have a clearer idea of our spiritual nature and what life is truly about. I think the book perhaps adds to that clarity. Actually the insights in this book, plus even more insights, are all coming into the culture at the same time, and many people are having these insights.

**David:** In your author's note in the front of the book, you say, "A new consciousness has been entering the human world, a new awareness that can only be called transcendent, spiritual . . . . At this moment in history, we seem attuned to the life process." What is special about right now?

**James:** Well, I think we're waking up to the full spiritual dimension of life. The modern age has been focused on achieving a kind of material, secular security and on developing technology. And now we're waking up to the mysterious aspects of life again and trying to come up with our own understanding of what is.

How should I understand this life of mine? How should I understand the spiritual dimension of my life? How can I make the world a better and more spiritual place?

**Gay Lynn:** What changes do you see happening around the world that show a new consciousness of love, a oneness, a positive change taking place?

**James:** What has happened in Eastern Europe and Russia is certainly an incredible, miraculous thing. Those people were willing to give up a whole approach to life because it was not fulfilling. They're moving back toward spirituality.

At the same time, much of the world looks like it's become more negative. But that's really the collapse of an old way of life, an old point of view. The old way suddenly does not suffice anymore; it doesn't give us fulfillment. And people are very frustrated and acting that out in all kinds of violent ways.

> **At the same time, much of the world looks like it's become more negative. But that's really the collapse of an old way of life, an old point of view. The old way suddenly does not suffice anymore; it doesn't give us fulfillment. And people are very frustrated and acting that out in all kinds of violent ways.**

Yet at the same time that's going on, there's this undercurrent of love and connection with the Divine that I think is just fully coming to consciousness in the '90s. And it's going to be, in my view, a transformative way that circles the globe.

**Gay Lynn:** You've said that our lives are meant to be miraculous. You seem to define or include in your understanding of miraculous the whole experience of synchronousness, which is what Carl Jung called . . .

**James:** . . . the perception of meaningful coincidence—when two things happen that seem beyond chance, when they seem to be reinforcing something in us and also seem to be pulling us along toward a certain destiny.

For example, you have a question, and you happen upon a book that answers that question. You need a new job, and mysteriously you run into just the opportunity you were looking for. There's a mystical side of life. It's the way the spirit operates. Our best destiny can come forward if we know how to take advantage of the opportunities that come synchronistically our way.

As we awaken to a more clarified approach to spirituality, a new spiritual world view as I like to call it, we begin to understand how to get out of our own way, how to let our best destiny come forward.

**David:** One character in your book has the opportunity to send energy to somebody. Could you talk a little bit about that?

**James:** What we're understanding right now is our wholeness and the power we have as spiritual beings. We have all this energy at our disposal once we make the connections to our own divinity. And we can use this energy intentionally. We can focus this energy on another human being in a conversation, speak to his or her higher self, speak to the place within.

And they feel uplifted and receptive. Then what usually happens is they share something with us that answers a question that we had. If we uplift people with enough energy, answers will come to us.

**David:** And sometimes we might not converse with them at all. We might see them on the subway or on the freeway or in a gathering somewhere, and we may just send them energy?

**James:** That's right. And the more we send out, the more we receive. That's not just a nice cliché, that's a spiritual fact; that's how it works.

**David:** You said that you are most frequently asked how much of this adventure really happened?

**James:** That's right. It's a parable. It's on the fiction list.

We have come through the '70s and '80s and find ourselves here in the '90s on a spiritual path, except that I have been motivated intensely by a need for clarity. I just tried to clarify my spiritual path by exploring how we begin to pull together all those loose ends from modern physics and interpersonal psychology and Eastern mysticism and the traditional religions that we've grown up with. The book is really the culmination of my trying to understand what is happening in this historical period. My conclusion is that humankind wants to experience spirituality as never before.

**David:** So, you put this in the form of an adventure story?

**James:** Yes, it allowed me to illustrate some of the concepts that I was seeking to convey. I call it an adventure parable.

**Gay Lynn:** Then this adventure parable is an ancient way of communicating truth—by parable or sacred mythology?

**James:** Exactly. It's fascinating to see people who have had no prior experience with anything, other than their own church perhaps, finding something in the book that clarifies some things for them.

**David:** Was there an activity or experience that sustained you during the writing of the book?

**James:** While working on the book, I lived in Birmingham, Alabama, worked as a therapist and regularly attended Unity of Birmingham. It is a very special place, a nurturing kind of place. The minister, Jerry Bartholow, and his wife Jane have created a very loving atmosphere where you can just come and get charged. It was very important in terms of my energy level to get this book done.

**David:** How autobiographical is the book? Is it you?

**James:** Well, it's me in the sense that this has been the core of the experiences that I've had. Much of the setting and the characters are composites. It's just meant to be a parable. I wanted to lay these ideas out as an effort toward clarity. It's intended for people to see what rings true for them and what doesn't.

**Gay Lynn:** How has writing the book transformed your life?

**James:** It's certainly been a validation. We've had our share of dead ends with this book. But once I got the message in the right shape, everything else was provided. It was just one synchronistic experience after another—from getting the book on paper, to getting it edited, to publishing the first edition, to running into the right publisher to take it worldwide. It's certainly been an awe-inspiring experience to watch all this unfold.

We've had such good word-of-mouth circulation for the book. People read, like the idea, and decide to send it to someone else—a family member, a friend, to whomever they think might like it or be helped by it. This is not a book made by the mass media. We haven't been on television shows; they didn't make this book. It went to number one on the bestselling list strictly because people out there decided it was a book they wanted to pass along.

**David:** So it's the power of the ideas and the possibilities these ideas offer that have made the book successful. And, obviously, you don't have to go to the Holy Land or India or Peru to find the nine insights.

**James:** Certainly the kind of truth we're talking about is within, but if one chooses to look for sacred sites, they're absolutely everywhere.

**David:** You're writing a continuation of the book now?

**James:** That's right. It's a direct sequel entitled *The Tenth Insight.*

**David:** Your life has been characterized by taking courageous action, by going beyond believing in or agreeing with something.

**James:** I'll put it in a little different way. It's not just about vision or talent or even opportunity. It's about persistence. Sometimes, when you think you have the Truth, you run into a brick wall. So you must figure out the lesson and why it's not working the way you intended. Then you shift it and evolve it until it's the Truth for you.

> **You know, when we meet that stranger for the third time in one week, we need to act on that. We have to strike up a conversation in some manner because what that connection might do is open the very door that we need opened.**

When that happens, your life is going to flow synchronistically, with meaningful coincidences, mysterious events. We just have to keep looking until we figure out that they are happening. You know, when we meet that stranger for the third time in one week, we need to act on that. We have to strike up a conversation in some manner because what that connection might do is open the very door that we need opened.

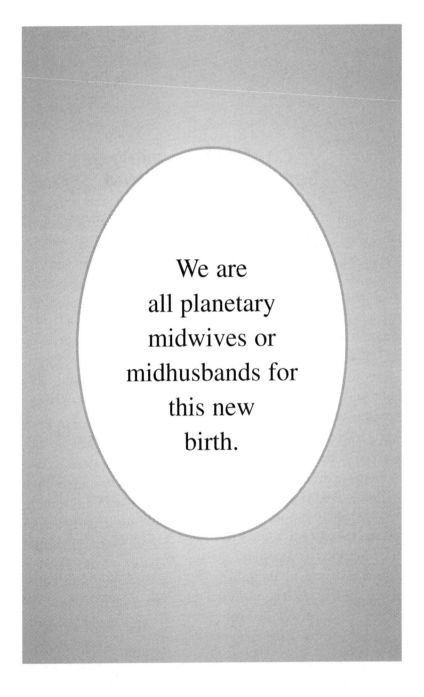

We are
all planetary
midwives or
midhusbands for
this new
birth.

# Co-Creating, with Barbara Marx Hubbard

Barbara Marx Hubbard is a world-famous futurist, speaker, and chairperson of worldwide conferences of scientists, scholars, and activities. Robert Muller, former United Nations Assistant Secretary General, once wrote of Barbara, "If I have ever met a person who is fully conscious of her responsibilities toward the earth, humanity and the cosmos, it is certainly Barbara Marx Hubbard. She is a true 21st-century woman."

The late Gene Roddenberry, creator of *Star Trek,* wrote, "Renowned as a futurist, Barbara Marx Hubbard also plants her feet firmly in *today.* In fact, her wit and wisdom always seem to be saying, 'The best way to get anywhere is to start from where you are.' I am grateful for the many things I have learned from her."

Buckminster Fuller, inventor and architect, once said, "There is no doubt in my mind that Barbara Marx Hubbard, who helped to introduce the concept of futurism to society, is the best informed human now alive regarding futurism and the foresights it has produced."

We interviewed Barbara in her lovely California home, sipped herbal tea, and reflected on the future and how we all play a major part in the evolutionary scheme of the planet.

**Barbara Marx Hubbard**

**Gay Lynn:** We are looking at our life as a continual birthing. You have written much using this metaphor. What do you see as a futurist?

**Barbara:** My metaphor for our story of creation is that creation is a birth. I see that our story is one of the birth of a planetary humanity. It took 15 to 20 billion years to create a planetary system that is awakening to itself as one body.

We are the generation born when the planet as a whole is awakening. We are the first generation to be aware that we are affecting the planet by everything we do. Nobody knows how to become responsible for a planetary system. There are no schools for conscious evolution except small, little pockets we are creating.

When I went to college, the great universities did not even recognize the planet was evolving, much less think about where it was going, and how to manage it!

> **We are the generation born when the planet as a whole is awakening. We are the first generation to be aware that we are affecting the planet by everything we do. Nobody knows how to become responsible for a planetary system. There are no schools for conscious evolution except small, little pockets we are creating. When I went to college, the great universities did not even recognize the planet was evolving, much less think about where it was going, and how to manage it!**

**David:** So what you are saying is that we are the planetary midwives or midhusbands for this new birth?

**Barbara:** I am coming at this from the perspective of being a planetary midwife, assuming that this is a normal birth, a normal event. I have not seen another planet go through this process, but I am assuming that it is not completely freakish in the universe for a planet to produce intelligent life. There may be a normal organic development of a planet. Just as there is a biological life cycle from conception to maturation, so there must be a planetary life cycle. It starts at the origin of creation and gestates through the formation of Earth, life, animal life, and human life—and now us. We are becoming a planetary species, suffering our birth pangs, recognizing that we are one body and must coordinate ourselves as a whole system.

We have reached the limits to growth on this planet. We are the last generation to reproduce up to maximum. One more doubling of our population would result in more than 10 billion people. The population cannot double again. That means in our generation, women and men will have fewer children, whether by choice or by catastrophe. Any culture that cannot control its population will be decimated.

**Gay Lynn:** So, if we are not reproducing ourselves up to maximum, how can we positively use this creative and regenerative power in another way?

**Barbara:** This brings us to the importance of creativity. That, I think, is the true result of this natural crisis. It is natural to hit a pollution limit. It is natural to reach a population limit. It is natural to shift from maximum procreation to co-creation. The energy of procreation and massive reproduction is beginning to shift in the developed world. In women, particularly, it is experienced as the desire for self-expression, life purpose, meaningful work. Sexual energy is shifting from the desire to reproduce oneself to a deeper desire to evolve oneself. Sexual energy is expanding to suprasexual energy. In sexuality, we join our genes to reproduce ourselves. In suprasexuality, we join our *genius* to express our untapped creativity. The joining of genius, like sex, is exciting, pleasurable. Nature has built in a great incentive to self-evolution, just as she did for self-reproduction! It feels wonderful to co-create.

So, we are moving from self-reproduction to self-evolution, from procreation, or reproducing yourself, to co-creation, or giving birth to the unique self through creative self-expression and vocation.

**David:** And since we are living longer lives, we have more time to evolve the self.

**Barbara:** Yes. The average lifespan at the turn of the last century was below the age of 50. Now it is inching up to 80. All of us over 50 are part of the new generation. In the past, we would have been dead. The meaning of longevity is to give us time to grow up. We don't know the full potential of the species.

When you think of having five to 10 children and dying at age 35—I mean, 35 to 40 was the average lifespan! I did not even wake up to who I was until I was 35. I had five children. Ordinary people died by then in the last century.

**Gay Lynn:** So much of the time, energy, nurturing, and love it took to raise large families is available for us to evolve ourselves and help evolve the planet.

**Barbara:** We are having a crisis of unexpressed creativity. There are very few outlets for our passionate desire to express ourselves in life purpose. We understand having children, but what about the urge to birth ourselves and to find a chosen vocation? We are not taught to seek our unique genius and express it in the world. You don't get hired for it. Usually our creativity has no job title. This desire for a more meaningful life often feels like frustration. What is wrong with me? Why am I not content? What is going on? A new archetype is being born—the co-creative person—one who is activated from within toward full self-actualization and self-realization.

In the rise of the co-creative person, the first step is the awakening of our greater growth potential. It is important to affirm this potential as good rather than as neurotic—as it was considered when I was 30.

> **We understand having children, but what about the urge to birth ourselves and to find a chosen vocation? We are not taught to seek our unique genius and express it in the world. You don't get hired for it. Usually our creativity has no job title. This desire for a more meaningful life often feels like frustration. What is wrong with me? Why am I not content? What is going on?**

I thought I was sick. The current view was: "You have five children. Why do you want to do more?"

**Gay Lynn:** I also experienced this same challenge in my life. I had a husband, two children, a home in the suburbs, and was asked, "Why isn't this enough? Why do you always want more?" I had to make some tough decisions at the time and the marriage ended.

**Barbara:** Yes. Women are being activated from within by

a passionate desire for self-expression and vocation. This urge is vital to planetary evolution, for within the untapped feminine creativity lies the intuition of what needs to be done to heal and evolve the world. The result of this shift from procreation to co-creation is that women and men have time to give birth to themselves—to nurture and mature unique creativity, to self-evolve rather than self-sacrifice for the sake of the child. Now we self-actualize for the sake of the world. For what the world needs is *not* more children, but wiser people.

This shift toward self-expression stimulates us to deepen our own inner knowing. We open our hearts, and out of that deep heart-knowing we find the thread of our own potential and commit to the birth of ourselves, just as we commit to the birth of a child. Very few of us have really given birth to ourselves—there has not been the time, the affluence, the education. In fact, this opportunity to mature and express ourselves as co-creative persons is the purpose of modern society. For all its destructiveness, its constructive side involves freeing millions of men and women to seek personal, spiritual and social growth. We are growing a crop of co-creative humans!

It takes commitment to mature ourselves. Even at the age of 64, I still feel like I am at the beginning. It is not that I feel young—I feel *new,* and newer and newer all the time. The planetary system is in the process of transformation to the next stage of evolution. We are entering into a period of radical newness. As members of the planetary body, we are becoming newer everyday.

Perhaps we are like cells in the body of a biological organism being born from womb to world. This is a disorienting change for the cells; they must begin new functions.

So now in our planetary body, we are being called to new tasks, greater responsibilities, amazing new possibilities.

I say to my cells, "Hang in there cells, we are by no means ready to leave. We have only barely begun, and it has taken us this long to get to this point!" I think Charles Fillmore, the co-founder of Unity, was right. We are moving toward regeneration. The time for regeneration on the planet is now. Regeneration begins to occur when our genius is activated through creativity. We are "turned on."

I believe that life purpose and regeneration are connected. If we have no desire for further creativity, degeneration occurs. But regeneration occurs spontaneously. Ultimately I believe we will learn to die by choice—and to live on by choice. We will live as long as we have a passion to create.

> I say to my cells, "Hang in there cells, we are by no means ready to leave. We have only barely begun, and it has taken us this long to get to this point!" I think Charles Fillmore, the co-founder of Unity, was right. We are moving toward regeneration. The time for regeneration on the planet is now. Regeneration begins to occur when our genius is activated through creativity. We are "turned on."

**Gay Lynn:** I am 40, and you are modeling a whole new way for me to look at my life and how to approach my 60s.

**Barbara:** Particularly after menopause, women seem to be regenerating and evolving rapidly instead of degenerating and dying rapidly. Perhaps menopause signals metamorphosis. We no longer have to produce eggs and reproduce the species. We have the time and energy to produce initiatives that contribute to the larger community.

The woman is awakening to a new function. She is becoming a co-creative woman. She has existed under the surface of society throughout history. But now she is arising by the millions—because it was time. The culture of the past would not allow it. The patriarchy held the power. But now, as we enter the time of partnership, as Riane Eisler would put it, there is a profound social need for the emergence of the co-creative woman. All our social systems are breaking down: health care, education, government. We must apply the creativity of woman to the evolution of communities and social systems in which our children can live and grow.

Within the co-creative woman is a code for the conscious evolution of humanity. When a woman finds her own deeper life purpose, that purpose is needed for the evolution of the planet. In her genius lies some contribution needed in the community. A co-creative woman is not trying to be equal with men. She is not, in general, attempting to successfully enter into existing structures. She seeks to create new structures, new systems, social innovations that enhance life.

**David:** How does that affect our relationships, our marriages, our partnerships?

**Barbara:** This leads to the great challenge of the man-woman relationship. It is utterly unprecedented for women en masse to rise up in this way. This is a bio-evolutionary shift of the first order. My partner and I are studying a model of the cosmic couple, outlined by Catherine Chardin. She points out that every embodied woman has a

Divine Masculine in her, and every embodied man has a Divine Feminine in him. As we move into the co-creative coupling between man and woman, the woman experiences vocational arousal. She is excited by her own potential. She follows her deep life purpose and births herself. This drive for self-expression often unbalances her relationship with a man, because it so easily feels to him like rejection. He may become hostile and the woman then feels rejected, and often is rejected when she expresses her power.

In the first phase of the women's movement, this drive for identity was aggressive. It seemed antagonistic, and often had to be. However, as we shift toward the cosmic couple, something new happens. The woman's drive, her "logos," deeply needs to be received by the feminine aspect of the man. Instead of being rejected repeatedly, she longs to be loved for her initiative.

> **As we move into the co-creative coupling between man and woman, the woman experiences vocational arousal. She is excited by her own potential. She follows her deep life purpose and births herself. This drive for self-expression often unbalances her relationship with a man, because it so easily feels to him like rejection. He may become hostile and the woman then feels rejected, and often is rejected when she expresses her power.**

**David:** So the first phase of the new coupling is not for the women to become more like men, but instead to be received by them.

**Barbara:** In the first phase of the cosmic couple, the Divine Masculine aspect of the woman is received in love by the Divine Feminine aspect of the man. Then the woman loves the man for his receptivity. Then the man, instead of rejecting his own feminine side and having to be super-masculine to survive in the competitive world, can honor his own feminine.

Much of what men have done was in support of the women who bore their children. They had to be strong, to protect, to defend, to fight, to bring home the money in the competitive world. It was not a one-way thing; the patriarchy in part evolved to support women—and then it went berserk! It became unbalanced and began to threaten not only women, but the whole world—whether through nuclear accident or environmental collapse.

> **Much of what men have done was in support of the women who bore their children. They had to be strong, to protect, to defend, to fight, to bring home the money in the competitive world. It was not a one-way thing; the patriarchy in part evolved to support women—and then it went berserk!**

So when the woman rises up with this passion to create and is received in love by the man, she loves him for his nurturing feminine side. He then begins to honor it, and that balances his masculine aspect with his feminine. Conversely, the woman's feminine side is balanced as she expresses her masculine initiative in the world.

**Gay Lynn:** How does the man feel if he is just supporting the woman in her achievements and not expressing his own creativity in some way?

**Barbara:** If the man is only supporting the woman, he can begin to feel insubstantial. He can feel at a loss with such a woman. So it is absolutely vital that the woman be attracted to the unexpressed creativity of the man and draw it out. Men often could not express their intuitive, creative sides in the competitive, masculine world. The world out there is tough, and it does not allow for deeper sensitivity of the male. It is often dangerous to be vulnerable.

So, as the woman feels received and loved for her strength, in return she loves the man's unexpressed creativity and creates a context in which he brings out his unexpressed masculine creativity, as he is nurturing hers.

**David:** So the new man is being brought forth in partnership with the new woman.

**Barbara:** Yes, and often the context in which the new man comes forth is set by the new woman. It is difficult for this whole man to emerge in a competitive, commercial society. And we can see that our current competitive systems are not serving us well in the realms of education, politics, and economics. We feel this in our Western world, the Communist world has already collapsed, and the Third World nations have social structures that are inadequate. Once again, this breakdown of the old structures is natural at the time of a planetary birth. And we can see even now that out of the breakdowns come many breakthroughs—social innovations in health, education, environment, management—that enhance personal responsibility, cooperation, creativity, sustainability.

I feel that the co-creative relationship between the whole woman and the whole man forms the basic unit of the emerging culture. The new family unit—the co-creative family—is emerging out of the breakup of the procreative family. The purpose of the co-creative family is to give birth to the full potential of each partner, and to the chosen child.

**Gay Lynn:** So all of this requires that the woman is honored and received for both her passion of creativity and her nurturing maternal feminine. Then she does not become overly driven from her masculine side.

**Barbara:** She maintains a high level of both aspects of her nature. Her masculine is being expressed through her vocation, and her feminine is being ignited to bring forth the creativity in the man. You see, it is really beautiful, theoretically. But it is one thing to say this; it is another thing to do it! As couples explore this challenging process together and support one another in achieving a new social pattern, the result will be a restructuring of society. When the man-woman relationship moves to a co-equal, co-creative partnership model, the new world will be stabilized and aggression will be converted to creative expression.

> The society that would evolve from co-equal, co-creative couples is a new world. The Divine knowing in the feminine in partnership with a whole man is, I believe, the guide to the evolution now.

**David:** Our society can evolve in a much different way as we stop the suppression of the feminine in ourselves and the domination of women in general. That can guide us all to a new birth of the whole planet.

**Barbara:** Yes. The society that would evolve from co-equal, co-creative couples is a new world. The Divine knowing in the feminine in partnership with a whole man is, I believe, the guide to the evolution now.

**David:** At mid-life you birthed a whole new life. Carl Jung talked about this, saying that the first half of life is not lived in the same way as the second half. There is a mid-life crisis, a birth, a questioning that takes place.

**Barbara:** Yes, that's very good. I, like so many millions of women, am giving birth to a new world. I began this second life in my mid-30s when I had a peak experience. I felt the Earth as one living body struggling to coordinate itself as a whole. This experience revealed my vocation: "Go tell the story of our birth, *Barbara.*" I found my vocation. Vocation is the passageway to the second life. It is our calling, our innate blueprint activating us to fulfill our potential. This could only happen when we have fewer children and live longer lives. As I said, this shift is a natural element of a natural planetary crisis or birth.

There seems to be a pause in the women's movement because much has been achieved, and even though much more must be achieved in the way of equal rights, the planetary shift is so great that women no longer want to be merely equal with what is dying. Equal rights is the *basis* for what we need to co-create a world equal to our potential.

**Gay Lynn:** How are the younger women doing in this time of great change?

**Barbara:** Younger women don't want to have to wait for their mid-life crisis. Many 20-year-olds already know they will not be satisfied by marriage and children alone. They know they must find a fulfilling vocation. Yet, a young woman turned on by her own vocation has a hard time finding the man who is willing to embrace her in that vocation. It is not easy for a woman of high creative passion to know how to relate to a man who still wants her to be his wife and support system. Even worse, the man does not know how to relate to her! Relationship and vocation may appear incompatible. They are not—but it requires excellent communication skills and deep compassion on the part of both partners.

I talk to a lot of young couples who are in trauma. It always helps for me to say to them, "I am just starting on this myself." The genetic code does not guide us in co-creative relationships; our instincts don't guide us. Our instincts tell us to submit to the man, to hold onto him. Suddenly our newer instinct is telling us to evolve ourselves. Then it actually seems like a terrible choice in some cases, and it may be very painful. These are all positive crises. They are part of the crisis of our planetary birth. The breakup of the nuclear family is giving us the opportunity to develop new forms of co-equal partnership.

**David:** What kind of pragmatic indications show that a new world, a new conscious evolution, is coming?

**Barbara:** There are many. The environmental movement. The ecological consciousness is fostering an understanding that we are connected to the whole system, that we are members of one body, that we are all relatives. This entire movement is only 30 years old. The environmental crisis is forcing us to learn how to manage a whole planetary ecology. This is an evolutionary drive of the highest order.

There is a massive revolution in health. We are learning to take responsibility for diet, exercise, attunement, prayer, self-healing. We are seeking alternative therapies that are nonintrusive. Millions of people have stopped smoking, and eat less or no red meat. Many people are becoming vegetarians, taking responsibility for their bodies as well as the larger environment.

Another positive sign is the movement from patriarchy to partnership. The quest for compassionate, noncoercive relationships. There is an evolution of religion itself, as we learn that we are co-creators with the process of creation, that our thoughts create our own reality.

It is a joy to find myself in the midst of such a mass movement. Because when we started 30 years ago, we felt pretty much alone. Today we don't feel alone at all! We are dealing with a mass awakening, a human development revolution. This revolution of human creativity, combined with environmental and social responsibility, along with proper use of advanced technologies, could lead to a quantum jump in our species' capacities. I believe we are actually transforming from a terrestrial, self-conscious phase to a universal, cosmic, conscious phase of human evolution. We are becoming physically and spiritually a co-creative humanity.

## Within

I read a map once
Saying the Kingdom of God
Was within me,
But I never trusted
Such unlikely ground.

I went out.
I scoured schools
And libraries
And chapels and temples
And other people's eyes
And the skies and the rocks,
And I found treasures
From the Kingdom's treasury,
But not the Kingdom.

Finally,
I came in quiet
For a rest
And turned on the light.

And there,
Just like a surprise party,
Was all the smiling royalty,
King, Queen, court.

People have been
Locked up for less, I know.

But I tell you
Something marvelous
Is bordered by this skin:

I am a castle
And the Kingdom of God
Is within.

PICTURE WINDOW
BY CAROL LYNN PEARSON

# READER/CUSTOMER CARE SURVEY

If you are enjoying this book, please help us serve you better and meet your changing needs by taking a few minutes to complete this survey. Please fold it & drop it in the mail.

**Name:** _____

**Address:** _____

_____

**Tel. #** _____

**(1) Gender:** 1) ____ Female  2) ____ Male

**(2) Age:** 1)____ 18-25  4)____ 46-55
2)____ 26-35  5)____ 56-65
3)____ 36-45  6)____ 65+

## (3) Marital status:

1)___ Married  3)___ Single  5)___ Widowed
2)___ Divorced  4)___ Partner

**(4) Is this book:** 1)____ Purchased for self?
2)____ Purchased for others?
3)____ Received as gift?

## (5) How did you find out about this book?

1)____ Catalog      2)____ Store Display
Newspaper
3)____ Best Seller List
4)____ Article/Book Review
5)____ Advertisement
Magazine
6)____ Feature Article
7)____ Book Review
8)____ Advertisement
9)____ Word of Mouth
A)____ T.V./Talk Show (Specify) _____
B)____ Radio/Talk Show (Specify) _____
C)____ Professional Referral _____
D)____ Other (Specify) _____

## Which Health Communications book are you currently reading? _____

As a special **"Thank You"** we'll send you exciting news about interesting books and a valuable Gift Cerfificate.
*It's Our Pleasure to Serve You!*

## (6) What subject areas do you enjoy reading most? (Rank in order of enjoyment)

1)____ Women's Issues/     5)____ New Age/
Relationships                  Altern. Healing
2)____ Business Self Help  6)____ Aging
3)____ Soul/Spirituality/   7)____ Parenting
Inspiration             8)____ Diet/Nutrition/
4)____ Recovery                      Exercise/Health

## (14) What do you look for when choosing a personal growth book?

(Rank in order of importance)
1)____ Subject          3)____ Author
2)____ Title            4)____ Price
Cover Design        5)____ In Store Location

## (19) When do you buy books?

(Rank in order of importance)
1)____ Christmas
2)____ Valentine's Day
3)____ Birthday
4)____ Mother's Day
5)____ Other (Specify _____

## (23) Where do you buy your books?

(Rank in order of frequency of purchases)
1)___ Bookstore        6)___ Gift Store
2)___ Price Club       7)___ Book Club
3)___ Department Store  8)___ Mail Order
4)___ Supermarket/      9)___ T.V. Shopping
Drug Store          A)___ Airport
5)___ Health Food Store

## Additional comments you would like to make to help us serve you better.

_____

_____

Thank You !!

FOLD HERE

**NO POSTAGE
NECESSARY
IF MAILED
IN THE
UNITED STATES**

# BUSINESS REPLY MAIL
FIRST CLASS MAIL  PERMIT NO 45  DEERFIELD BEACH, FL

POSTAGE WILL BE PAID BY ADDRESSEE

HEALTH COMMUNICATIONS
3201 SW 15TH STREET
DEERFIELD BEACH, FL 33442-9875

# 3

# Music and the Spirit

# Music: Poetry to Our Souls

Discovering the mystical aspects of life requires a completely unique and different approach. We cannot study the Feminine—the magnetic, birthing energy—in the same way we have studied everything else in our lives. We have been taught to analyze, dissect, rationalize, order, and intellectually articulate all aspects of the Masculine energies. These quantifiable methods are valuable for some studies, but not for the mystical part of our being that is touched in a different way, much like the experience of listening to music. We surrender to music and are transformed by the vibrational tones, melodies, and lyrics which become poetry to our souls.

We are profoundly affected by the sounds around us. The trickle of a water fountain soothes and calms us in our own home. Gay Lynn enjoys playing guitar and singing chants and songs, and this act of love has inspired her children to discover their own talents. All of us have moments when a special song comes on the radio and transports us to another time and place. Many veterans of war have recalled that certain songs kept them going when all seemed lost and in upheaval—the song in their head pulled them through. Music is truly a gift of God that we perhaps take for granted most of the time.

Many special holidays would not be the same without music. Christmas music sets the tone for that season; it evokes what we call the "Christmas Spirit."

King Saul sought solace and called for David and his harp. Likewise, when we are upset, music can be a balm for our souls. Yet some music has just the opposite effect: It wakes us up, gets us moving, puts a bounce in our step. Just as different foods affect the body in different ways, different music can also profoundly affect our bodies.

We all have had the experience of hearing a song so beautiful, sung in a manner that caused the hair to rise on our arms and shivers to go up and down our spines. We are made up of energy; electromagnetic activity takes place within and around us. Music and sound interact with our body systems, creating electrochemical responses. We could say that we have "sound-health" and allow sound to facilitate the birthing of our soul experience. We are learning more today about how music, sound and the body work in harmony to relieve stress, lower blood pressure and enhance sexual relations.

Today we have music therapy, which has its origin in ancient times. In their book, *Healthy Pleasures,* Robert Ornstein and David Sobel describe the oldest known medical document as a papyrus containing incantations used to heal the sick. They observe, "To the ancient Greeks, Apollo was the god of both medicine and music. Early physicians used music to regulate heartbeat, and music and singing were traditionally used to cure many ailments, including 'melancholia.'" They emphasize that healing with sound and rhythm is widely accepted in many cultures throughout the world.

The lyrics and sound of music nourish our souls and bodies. We are fed with words of hope, love and faith. We long to experience the Divine presence, and often that experience is enhanced through the gift of music.

Hear Spirit
sing to you:
"You are
so beautiful
to me."

*Los Angeles, California*

# Music as a Form of Ministry, with O. C. Smith and Robbie Smith

O.C. and Robbie Smith serve together in a spiritual work they call the City of Angels Church of Religious Science near Los Angeles International Airport. O.C. speaks to a congregation of great numbers each Sunday, and we were royally welcomed when we spoke there. The Sunday service features some of O.C.'s friends who are jazz artists and members of The Sunday Morning Band. They play a piece in the middle of the service, adding their unique talents to the joy and celebration.

O.C. made his mark in music during the 1970s. Now he has completed the transformation from pop singer to spiritual leader. When he came to perform in Detroit, he always visited us on Sundays and sometimes sang in the service. One Mother's Day, he sang "You Are So Beautiful to Me" to a tearful congregation. We talked to O.C. and Robbie in their gracious home in Los Angeles, where they told their beautiful story of love and service.

**Gay Lynn:** O.C., can you share a little about your evolution from recording artist to ministry in your City of Angels church?

**O.C.:** Those that study the principles of life know that the giant oak is already contained in the tiny acorn. And so it

**O.C. and Robbie Smith**

was in my life. That which I am now was always in the
seed of the music.

To give you an example, all the songs I have ever sung
that were hit songs, like "Honey," "For the Good Times,"
"Don't Misunderstand"—there is a list of them. I didn't
realize it at the time on a conscious level, but they were a

form of ministry. So I was evolving to where I am now and didn't realize it. So many things that happened have prepared the way and led me to the life I am now fortunate enough to be living. What I was doing in my singing career was ministering for years through the music.

I have had hundreds of people from various walks of life come up to me and share their stories about the music and how it affected them.

**David:** What are some of your favorites?

**O.C.:** Songs like "Daddy's Little Man" and "Son of Hickory Hollow's Tramp," "Help Me Make It Through the Night," and "Little Green Apples" came out through the early '70s when the Viet Nam war was going on. I have talked to many soldiers involved in the conflict who said there was a particular song that helped them through, because the lyrics held so much meaning for them. The song helped them deal with their emotions and remain centered and gave them a reason to go on and get out of that tough situation. As the war raged on, the songs gave them a degree of sanity, because it was something they could truly relate to.

Another example was when Robbie and I were at a function one evening, and a couple came up to us and shared that they had three daughters and all three were conceived by "Little Green Apples"! [Laughter.]

All the music was a form of ministry; it's no different now. To me, this is the most powerful time in my life. Back then I was not consciously aware of what was going on in my life—now I am. I am aware of the power of the music and I am aware of the power of the teachings of Religious Science. It is precious to me to put both of these together— the music and the teaching in the work I am doing today.

**Gay Lynn:** What made you realize that you were on a spiritual journey?

**O.C.:** Meeting Robbie was a part of it. For the first time in my life I met someone I really felt deeply about, and it continues to grow. I was on a spiritual quest and searching. Robbie and I were at a party and the conversation got to religion. I had not been to a church for awhile—Sunday morning football was my church—but there was a searching going on inside me on a subconscious level. I have always been a person who related very deeply to love. It came through my music and everything I did. I have always loved people.

My spiritual parts weren't being addressed and yet I was exploring, going here and there. But I wasn't satisfied. We were sharing this at the party and a couple invited us to join them the next day at the Wilshire Ebell Theater, where Dr. Joseph Murphy was the teacher. We went in for an hour and he just spoke. And I went out on the steps of the theater—it was a beautiful summer day—and I said to myself I didn't know what the man said, but I knew whatever he said, I had to hear more of it. I had finally found what I was searching for and I know it was searching for me. We were drawn to each other. And from that moment I began to study and listen and read. I was obsessed.

I know now this was the transformational process happening in me. The seed was birthing forth and the greater me was beginning to manifest itself in the way Spirit had always intended me to be—moving me toward the ministry I am doing now.

I was a man with three loves: Robbie, Religious Science, and my music. They all came together: the relationship, the spiritual quest and my music—all significant happenings came together at one time. That was the transformative part of it, and yet at the time I was still not fully aware that my life was evolving so beautifully, with such meaning, purpose and direction. I know that today.

**Gay Lynn:** Robbie, it sounds like your relationship helped to nurture or provide the sacred space for the spiritual life to become more conscious.

**Robbie:** Well, it just didn't happen for him. It happened for both of us. Both of us had been previously married. I really don't believe you have to die to become a new person. You can describe this as spiritual evolution, being aware of Divine Intelligence, a raising in consciousness, or a rebirth. However we describe it, I know I am not the same person that I was 21 years ago. There was a quiet progression so that when O.C. and I came together, I knew what we were supposed to do. Both of us had planted spiritual seeds, and when we physically saw one another our consciousness knew that this was a special union. This was the beginning of a new level of our spiritual evolution at that time in our lives. This was a form of birth that was full of beautiful change, that was happening for both of us.

**David:** What was the process of labor and delivery of this new work that you have birthed together in City of Angels?

**O.C.:** As far as the church is concerned, it was like the method of delivery called Lamaze exercises, where there is little pain because you are working with the process. You just keep breathing—keep breathing! It was what Spirit wanted us to do so there was no pain in it at all. There have been some challenges, but Robbie and I combined our talents to birth a beautiful, growing ministry.

Let the music
we listen to be for
sound health.

*San Anselmo, California*

# Delivering the Symphony of Life, with Steven Halpern

Steven Halpern has received international acclaim as one of the pioneers of New Age music. At the first International New Age Music Conference in February 1989, he was honored with a prestigious Crystal Award for his contribution to the field of contemporary instrumental music as a composer, multi-instrumentalist, recording artist, producer, and president of his own independent record label. Halpern's recordings are extremely popular, with global sales of over two million copies. But of all his accomplishments, Steven is most proud of his endeavors to reawaken an awareness of the true powers of music as a healing art form.

**Gay Lynn:** Steven, what are some practical ways we can balance the Divine Masculine and Divine Feminine energies in our lives?

**Steven:** Drumming activates Masculine and Feminine and bilateral hemispheric balance in the brain, even if you just use the right and left hands, tapping or clapping in syncopated patterns. *(Steven taps his hands on his legs in a steady beat, alternating right hand, left hand.)* Some

**Steven Halpern**

people have difficulty doing this. It is good to have a drum or other instruments around the house so you can have reflective sound opportunities.

Another kind of healing physical activity involves drumming and chanting together.

**David:** Matthew Fox says we have an affinity for the drum because we grew up next to one for the first nine months of life in our mothers' wombs.

**Gay Lynn:** How does music on the radio today affect us?

**Steven:** Songs on the radio today are based on the sound of a machine. The goal of heavy metal music in the 1970s was to make your drum sound like a piston in a car. In the same way, the blues first would make the rhythm sound like a railroad train going down the tracks. Now we have synthesizers, drum machines and robotics. There is nothing natural or normal for the heart to respond to because the rhythm will manipulate the heartbeat of the listener automatically. So if your heartbeat is forced to match a robot, that brings stress in right away. We always need to consider the source of our music. We have to take care of our own programming. Just like we have the right foods in the refrigerator, we need to have sound tracks available that are good for us.

> So if your heartbeat is forced to match a robot, that brings stress in right away. We always need to consider the source of our music. We have to take care of our own programming. Just like we have the right foods in the refrigerator, we need to have sound tracks available that are good for us.

**David:** We have talked about the Divine Darkness. How does this relate to our health and music for birthing the best of who we are?

**Steven:** When I compose, I meditate, and work close-eyed. That is where I find the deepest connection. In this Divine Darkness, I feel the greatest nurturing, renewing, and recharging when I go into these spaces.

Also, I typically compose at night, a time when there is a quiet outside as well as inside. When we close our eyes, we induce alpha waves between eight to 12 cycles per second. So much of our society is about keeping our eyes open, watching TV. In the 1960s, people would listen to music with their eyes closed. Now it's music television, MTV, and music videos, and people are listening to music, but they are watching something. I have rebelled at that situation.

I remind people that if you want to hear the music, you need to close your eyes; then you are able to get more out of the music, and get more into the music.

> When you cut off the visual stimulation, which is about 75 percent of the input from the senses, you open up a whole new range of consciousness. The stars are always in the sky, but the sun obliterates them. It is so important to take the time to close our eyes and listen to the music from that sacred space within. We get so much more into the music.

**Gay Lynn:** So we need to select a music track and listen in the Divine Darkness?

**Steven:** When you cut off the visual stimulation, which is about 75 percent of the input from the senses, you open up a whole new range of consciousness. The stars are always in the sky, but the sun obliterates them. It is so important to take the time to close our eyes and listen to the music from that sacred space within. We get so much more into the music.

**David:** In your long and distinguished career as a musician, composer, speaker, and business person, I am sure you have had your share of birth pains. How do you deal with them?

**Steven:** Oh, yes, I have had my share of birth pains. Last week we called the factory and the people there forgot to print our latest compact disc, and we got bumped out of rotation. It was going to take two weeks to a month to get back into production, and we had orders waiting. I took a deep breath and said a prayer: "It is in Divine Order." If it isn't—it isn't! I did everything I could to make it happen. I called some people at the factory and had it rescheduled, and then I had to "let go and let God" and release it. I did everything I could—used all the tools I had. I took responsibility for the part I could do, and then at a certain point, when I realized I had done everything I could, I had to surrender. Surrendering has always been a big teacher to me, and letting go and letting God—I think that is a big teacher to us all.

**Gay Lynn:** Now that you are married, there is a balance not only within your own Divine Feminine and Masculine, but also in the fulfillment of a relationship.

**Steven:** Yes, being in a more balanced place both within and with my wife gives me more fulfillment. We were told years ago that to sing the blues you have to be really poor. Or to play jazz music, you had to be really angry. I don't agree with this. A teacher once said to me, "Steven, you can play better music if you have had a full meal and you know where the rent money is!" That is different than coming from that experience of lack and nonprosperity.

So this whole process of birthing and being married is an expression of the abundance in my life, and it will feed into the music.

**David:** Many people listen to your music when they make love . . . .

**Steven:** People figured that out with *Spectrum Suite.* They said, "Well, this is music for relaxation and meditations so we should not make love to this." But, then they found out that when they get relaxed, there is a higher octave of loving. With the robotic music, they are working with the aggressive thrusting technology. With *Spectrum Suite* and the other tracks, there was an alignment of energy. The heart centers of the two became more in alignment and literally more in harmony. This energy and balance up-shifts the entire experience of lovemaking. And when you have seven chakras in alignment instead of two—well, it's better!

## Your Right Mind

To feed your right mind:
   Moonlight.
   Douse the lights, douse even the candle
   Speak to her gently; she's been shunned
     so long, she runs away.
   Suggest, don't expect
   Invite
   Wait

Let being fill up the space
   of doing
So that what you're doing
   is being.

 Let the message emerge
   from the sea of understanding
     like a mermaid singing her seduction.
Think fishes, flying through dark waters.
Think night, moonlit seas, and
   no moonlight at all.
   Think water. Think depths, dampness.
     Think subtle. Think subtler.
   Think feelings.

Your wis-dame, your wisdom,
   is an archivist. She knows what happened.
   Just ask.
   She isn't afraid, she's been here before.

Another kind of clarity, silvery, not stark, emerges.
　　Your wis-dame is your oldest ally,
　　your mother-wit.

Without her you are less than half yourself;
　　with her you are whole and ready.
Like a dolphin she is beside you
　　when you are goalless
and seeking only to satisfy your higher yearning.

Be attracted, addicted to life
　　and life's deeper demands.
Love, don't curse, the blind alleys
　　the red lights and lost luggage.
　　Without guessing there's no game.
Not "no pain no gain"
　　but "no love no gain."

Your mother-wit,
your wise dame
The sage speaks in patterns and pictures,
a scatter tongue. Catch as you can
　　her butterfly dust

But if you treasure her treasure
　　be loyal.
For eons she has been wooed in the dark
　　and spurned in the sun.
If she was with you then
　　she's with you now.

Ask
Ask
and then, of course,
　　　　　　　listen.

—*Marilyn Ferguson*

# 4

# Birthing the Soul of Business

We read an article in *Unity Magazine* (November 1994) entitled, "Business: The Old and New Stories," and knew we had to interview its author, Dr. Charles Garfield. We also knew we had to talk with entrepreneur Rinaldo Brutoco, one of the founders of the World Business Academy. When we arrived at the corporate headquarters of the Red Rose Collection and told Rinaldo we had been inspired by the Garfield article that *Unity Magazine* had reprinted from *Second to None,* he said, "That article parallels the World Business Academy work!" That synchronism seemed to confirm that these two men were important to interview in a growing body of business leaders, consultants, writers, conference leaders, and organizational development people concerned with new ways of working, doing business and prospering.

We present the Rinaldo Brutoco interview first because he and the Red Rose Collection, the company where he serves as president, demonstrate the principles and process that Charles Garfield outlines in his article. It works. Red Rose is not an isolated example of transformational business. It evolved from creative, courageous, adventurous thinking. Some will be scared, disbelieving and reactionary to Rinaldo's description of Red Rose. They might say, "But who's the boss?" Others may refuse to believe that there can be a holistic new way of living and working that actually applies spiritual ideals. Some will cling to their back-to-basics business fundamentalism, and others will be so impressed with the possibilities for mind change and organizational transformation that they will exclaim, "This is exciting! This newfound way of partnering and prospering unites, frees, inspires, motivates and helps us care for our ultimate home and bottom line—the Earth."

We would like to share a few key thoughts from Charles Garfield's article to introduce this subject of "Birthing the Soul of Business":

> *I think the role business must play in today's world is that of sacred stewardship for the common good. Where does this mission of sacred stewardship for the whole start? I think it starts with a new myth, a guiding ethic, a new story that explains how the world works, what we value, and who we are. At the heart of this new story are three values:*
> - *Exceptional service*
> - *Exceptional quality*
> - *Fulfilled people functioning at their best.*
>
> *The old paradigm of business in the industrial era was based on four powerful stories, all of which are leaving us. These four stories are also changing in our larger cultures.*
>
> *The first is the story of business and society as a finely tuned machine—the basic mechanical view of the world*

*. . . . In this machine view of the world, people are viewed as human widgets, disposable work units, factors of production, reduced to fractions of their potential.*

*The second story that's rapidly leaving us is the story of unlimited growth—economics disassociated from its ecological fabric. We treat the Earth as we treated the American Frontier of old—as if it were limitless . . . .*

*The third story rapidly leaving us is the story of hierarchy—pyramids, ladders—as the most efficient form of organization; command-control organizations characterized by the big boss at the top and armies of drone-line compliant workers below . . . .*

*The last story that's leaving us rapidly is the story of the lone pioneer, the rugged individualist . . . . These warriors enthusiastically recommend to the company that they get "lean and mean, cut to the bone, trim the fat," even if it means laying off thousands of workers.*

*These stories are all changing and the changes are very poignant clues to global mind change. First, the story of the machine is changing into the story of the ecosystem. Companies as ecosystems. Organizations as ecosystems . . . .*

*The story of unlimited growth is changing to the story of sustainable growth, healthy growth that doesn't jeopardize the prospects of the planet for future generations . . . .*

*Third, the story of hierarchy with a big boss at the top is changing to the story of the democratic networking organization. A networking organization operates more like a spider's web than a machine . . . .*

*We're seeing that there are two kinds of changes: reform and transformation. Reform is a change within the old paradigm, a change within the old system retaining the underlying assumptions.* Transformation involves a shift in the basic paradigm, a change in underlying assumptions. *After all, you can't make a light bulb out of a candle no matter what you do to it. Likewise you can't make an ecosystem out of a machine . . . .*

*Leaders in world business are becoming the first true planetary citizens, but they've got no vision of how a healthy planetary ecosystem works. The global mind change we speak of involves implanting at the heart of our institutions a humanistic perspective, a deep ecological ethic, and a profound spiritual basis.*

*What's needed is a vision that joins us to nature and to all that lives. Those transforming organizations embracing the new story are busy integrating the so-called masculine and feminine values. Feminine values such as caring, compassion, empathy, and tenderness are now given serious priority. And business is moving away from its blind attachment to hierarchical, exploitative, and dominator-based organizations associated with our most painful problems.*

*In reconciling, integrating, and bringing together these feminine and masculine values, business is slowly learning to be tough on the problems and tender on the planet and its inhabitants. As business becomes more complex, men and women in business have to learn to communicate with one another and cooperate in much more subtle ways. You can't put somebody on the moon unless you like your teammates and can work well in an interdependent context. The quality of our products, our work forces and our work places depends as never before on the quality of our relationships with one another . . . .*

*In our new story of business ecosystems we finally learned that it's not just wrong to exploit workers, it's stupid. You can't make high-quality products and deliver high-quality services with exploited workers. It will never happen. The old story told us that it didn't matter what you manufactured, as long as you pumped up its image with enormous feats of advertising. The new story talks to us about the need for authenticity, interdependence, integrity and keeping promises. New story beliefs that are critical to a business ecosystem are based on reverence for life. Central to the new story is the realization that at the heart of healthy economic and business growth is a theory of holism.*

*Burlingame, California*

# The Blooming of Red Rose, with Rinaldo Brutoco

Rinaldo Brutoco is chairman of the board, chief executive officer, president and chief operating officer of The Red Rose Collection, Inc. Rinaldo is also the chief executive officer at Dorason Corporation, a consulting and merchant banking firm. Dorason Corporation was founded in 1981 by Rinaldo as a merchant bank to seek investment opportunities in areas where a socially valuable contribution could be made to demonstrate the economic viability of "doing well by doing good." More specifically, it was created to "serve the feminine aspect of the Divine energies at this time on the planet." He founded the World Business Academy, and currently serves as both a director and trustee of that organization.

Lalla Shanna Brutoco is the vice president/merchandising and creative director of The Red Rose Collection. Her responsibilities include merchandise selection and the creative display of the merchandise in each catalog. Red Rose currently sends out 7.2 million catalogs a year. It has been placed three times on the *INC* 500 list of fastest growing privately held companies.

The Brutocos have two daughters in their 20s and a 10-year-old son. Two years ago, they adopted a Russian orphan

**Rinaldo Brutoco**

(now eight) from St. Petersburg. The seven-month adoption process culminated in a private meeting with Mikhail Gorbachev. Rinaldo is a member of the board of directors of Gorbachev Foundation/USA, a nonprofit, nonpartisan educational foundation created in 1992 to address the challenges of the post-Cold War world. The Foundation also channels funds to agencies that aid children.

We met Rinaldo in his office at Red Rose, located in an industrial park south of San Francisco. We saw him and his family the following day at their place of worship—the Unity Palo Alto Community Church—where we spoke.

Rinaldo's legal and business background, as well as his Spirit, blend well in his place of service. Nobel laureate Albert Schweitzer once said, "At that place in life where your talents meet the needs of the world, that is where God wants you to be." Rinaldo and Shanna have found that place.

**David:** We have looked for talismans, symbolic objects, art pieces that carry a spiritual or sacred meaning to use with people. We often pass around a stuffed heart, for instance, in our "Heart-to-Heart" ceremony to remind us to listen and share from our hearts. What you have done at Red Rose is collect hundreds of such objects of reverence, special clothes, artifacts, books, tapes, and offer them to millions of people.

**Rinaldo:** Yes, that's clearly intentional and that's why we call it "The Collection." When we started 10 years ago, the goal of all this was to find these types of objects. We first called it "Gifts of the Heart." Like you, we were also interested in that heart-to-heart connection, rather than trying to propound some metaphysical doctrine. We didn't see that as our job. After several years, we became aware that for a lot of people there was something else that needed to happen first. They were not even ready for their heart to open. That's when we started to look at rediscovering your own personal magic. We said, "Gee, how do people do that? If they have already accepted all the great lies that our society has propagated, what can we do to help?"

**Gay Lynn:** What would you consider some of the great lies?

**Rinaldo:** One great lie is that we live in a world of scarcity, when the truth is we live in a world of abundance. Other great lies are that we were born for struggle and pain; we are separate; we are competitive with one another; and what I do for a living is who I am as a being. Another is that it doesn't matter what you put in your head—that watching endless acts of violence doesn't brutalize us.

So we asked, "How do you blow on that little ember of Spirit in each person to make it glow, knowing that we are making the world we live in? How can we help people to become more aware of their personal power?"

We might put a pair of earrings with a moon and stars out there. What's that got to do with anything? A woman looks in the mirror and she gets an inkling that, "There is something about me that's a little bit cosmic." We're on the right track; that's blowing on the ember. Then we have other resources that can support people in greater explorations into their sense of wonder.

**David:** What is your goal as a company?

**Rinaldo:** We look for the places that people wanted to play, and then let people select their comfort zone for how alive they want to be. If they want to be really alive, they can read our magazine, *Catalist,* [sic] and find the philosophical underpinnings, the awarenesses that are behind our products. Maybe 20 percent of our 400,000 regular customers will do that. But that's okay, because the rest will find their own way to feed their soul. Of course, it may be that a magazine is not going to appeal to everyone in today's visually oriented society.

**Gay Lynn:** What do you see in the fable of "The Goose That Laid the Golden Eggs"?

**Rinaldo:** For us as men, particularly, there has been such a vigorous pursuit of performance that we are driven to demand more outcomes than it is prudent to ask of nature. Outcomes can only be created as a process. There was no gold as such inside the goose. It was an alchemical process by which the form of a golden egg was created and birthed.

**Gay Lynn:** The mother puts together all these elements to make bones, tissues, organs— just as we all do to make ourselves.

**Rinaldo:** Right. But rather than honoring that wonder in ourselves, we fixate on results alone and often on "bigger is better." That outcome-driven pressure that men often carry with them, particularly in Western society, is killing our ability to be with the process—to let something inner have importance and nurture it until it comes forth in its own right time.

At the same time, when I look at the metaphysical community, I'm concerned that there is an "addiction to process," that it becomes a substitute to ever getting the eggs made. I think it's a story that has a double meaning in modern times, and that is for those of us who are happy to see the goose cluck away and never produce an egg, a little prodding to the goose is not a bad idea as there ought to be an egg at the end of this process. And one a day seems like a good idea!

**David:** How did the birth of Red Rose take place?

**Rinaldo:** It really started out of *A Course in Miracles*. My wife and partner made these photographs of roses. We printed them up as a present for Judy Skutch because Judy was instrumental in bringing the Course to the world. So we used this quote from the Course: "Deep within you is everything that is perfect, ready to radiate through you and out into the world." And we framed them and gave them to Judy. Then Judy wanted sets to give to people at Christmas. We searched around the world to find these unusual frames that we had bought and could not find them, so we ended up making the frames ourselves. We had frames left over, and we announced the price. We had these in our garage.

**Gay Lynn:** This is kind of a miracle in itself.

**Rinaldo:** Yes. In six months we sold $25,000 of these rose pictures with the verses on them. We added a few other favorite tapes and books, such as the ultimate business book, *The Shamballa Warrior.* It went on as a cottage industry out of the garage. I finally had to make a decision. I was a lawyer involved in many nonprofit projects and for-profit companies. I was helping Shanna do the Red Rose project because I love her and wanted to support her. So, as I saw it, the artistic, feminine aspect of the Divine could emerge here. I just was in a supporting role so this creative, feminine expression of Lalla Shanna could get itself out into the marketplace.

So we meditated on this for quite some time, and what came through to me was that we could provide the highest service by proving conclusively that selling products like this is a business. That was a culmination for me in my career. If people like me, of my skills set, chose to sell only things that are ennobling and enlivening for people and the planet, and we chose to do it with the best business tools we are capable of bringing to the party, then I am fulfilling what I am meant to do with my life. And we are really committed to taking a service role. For example, it isn't my responsibility to create the content, but it is my responsibility to serve so this feminine consciousness can get out into the world. That is the highest calling for me as a businessman in my life. If we are so fortunate as to create a surplus—called a profit—then that would inspire initiative. At first, people would only copy us to make money, but if they are going to be successful, they really have to get into it. There is a good possibility they also will be touched inwardly and find an idealism beyond their materialism. At least I hope so.

**David:** So you and your wife are still partners in the work?

**Rinaldo:** Lalla Shanna is the keeper of the flame. I agreed to be the president and CEO on the condition that I not pick the products or decide how to display them. As president, I keep us operational. I make sure that when that 30-foot-high printing press needs to go, it's ready, and we get out those seven million catalogs and all else we print. This is not a top-down organization. I help people get things done, get it out there, make the systems work. And I love it. What holds us together are core values. That's what is in charge. We serve these core ideals. They provide the real direction. So when we need to know what to do, we go and meditate on these. Everyone works in teams.

**Gay Lynn:** Where did these core values come from?

**Rinaldo:** The core values are evolutionary in nature. I can tell you what some are, and others are still emerging. The ultimate core values which we have articulated are love, compassion, truth, integrity, empathy, joy—what Aldous Huxley called "perennial wisdom."

When we tried to first put these things down, a statement showed up on our bulletin board. We only had seven employees and none had put it there. We never found where it came from.

# A Message

Love and serve all humanity.
    Assist everyone.
Be cheerful. Be courteous.
Be a dynamo of irrepressible happiness.
See God and good in every face.
There is no saint without a past.
There is no sinner without a future.
    Praise every soul.
If you cannot praise someone
Let them pass out of your life.
    Be original. Be inventive.
Dare, dare, and then dare more.
Do not imitate. Stand on your ground.
Do not lean on the borrowed staff
    of others. Be yourself.
 All perfection and all virtues of the deity
    are hidden inside you.
    Reveal them.
The Savior also is already within you.
    Reveal him.
Let his grace emancipate you.
Let your life be that of a rose.
Though silent, it speaks in the language
    of fragrance . . .

*ANONYMOUS*

**Rinaldo:** Okay, message received! But then we had our first controversy in the company. What was the controversy about?

**Gay Lynn:** The Savior is a "he."

**Rinaldo:** Right. So we had to let it sit for a while. Do we use it, change it, not use it? We decided to go with it without changing it, and we humbly accepted what had come to us. It stopped being an issue. The way we're holding the statement these days is that the *him* they are talking about here is not one who has testosterone. It's the *him* side of our *herness,* because all the values and the rose itself are *herness.* So we print this up and send them to people. This is what we are. This is what we do. This is why we are here. What doesn't appear in this message is: Find out what's trendy this year and sell it.

**David:** Do you see this as a transformative business?

**Rinaldo:** This is maybe the world's first *business ashram,* an intentional community organized around spiritual principles. I explain to every new employee who comes into this community that this is the way it works at this stage of human history: "Everything that you're ready to come up against as your next level of growth is going to hit you right here. Your next big issue, me included, is going to come right to you and you have to make a choice. Do you want to break through to your next level of awareness, or do you want to stay with the level of pain you know that's comfortable? Two choices. And as soon as you break through, if you do, your reward is it will happen again, as long as you are in this intentional community."

**Gay Lynn:** Sounds like a birthing process.

**Rinaldo:** No question about it. It's labor pains. You're giving birth to your new self. So after you go down the birth canal with all the trauma, tenseness, tightness, constriction, and whatever else happens, you pop out. There's this new being. And if you're real good, you get to grow up real fast and give birth to yourself all over again. If you're not willing to go that fast, then you may get stuck in the birthing process or you stay barren for a time. That's okay, too. I tell you, every time I break through, I get confronted again and again and again. It's tough work. If I've had a bad day, I need to own it as my day and see that something is trying to reflect itself for me. My challenge is to understand what I need to break through so I can be reborn on that next level. God gives good clues!

> No question about it. It's labor pains. You're giving birth to your new self. So after you go down the birth canal with all the trauma, tenseness, tightness, constriction, and whatever else happens, you pop out. There's this new being. And if you're real good, you get to grow up real fast and give birth to yourself all over again.

**David:** Has God given you good clues?

**Rinaldo:** I know I'm in my right and perfect place. I'm thankful I'm able to give my gifts in such a fun and life-enhancing endeavor. I'm learning my lessons in truth daily.

We were the second-fastest growing catalog company in America for eight years. For awhile we lost our ability to hold it together spiritually, if you will. Not that we ever did anything inappropriate, but you could feel the spiritual energy not being in charge. Through the pain, confusion, and stress, we learned that just because you can do something doesn't mean you should do something. It wasn't healthy or right for us to try to do more than a wise stretch. I'm 49 and I've just learned to set healthy boundaries. It's one of my big lessons.

*In a profile of visionary business people, James E. Liebig found that aware leaders, such as the Brutocos, are finding viable strategies for:*

- *enhancing social equity;*
- *protecting the natural environment;*
- *fostering human creativity;*
- *serving higher purposes, including spiritual, service, and community values;*
- *behaving ethically, and*
- *providing transformational leadership.*

Merchants of Vision
*by James E. Liebig (Berrett-Koehler Publishers, San Francisco published in cooperation with the World Business Academy)*

# Thoughts from David:

## You Can't Hurry Mother Nature

There is an order and timing to birthing that we have to honor.

When I was a boy, my family lived on a farm in southern Michigan in the 1940s during a period when my father had to take an extended leave from his clinic because of X-ray burns he suffered. We had chickens on the farm and would get fresh eggs each day. Sometimes we let the hen sit on the eggs until they hatched into chicks.

I became impatient, waiting so long for those white and brown eggs to hatch, so I would go out sometimes and shake them out of curiosity to see what was happening, if anything. One day I decided to break open one of the eggs to help the chick get out so it didn't have to stay in there so long. Of course, I beheld a half-developed little bird which then could not continue its natural development.

I took the egg to the house and asked my mother what was going on. She kindly explained that I had to be patient and allow the egg time. Time and the warmth of the hen promotes a natural beneath-the-surface development. When the chick was ready, it would hatch. She said, "You can't hurry Mother Nature. She knows what she is doing."

I learned a valuable lesson that afternoon on the farm. I

can't say I have always been good at waiting for Mother Nature to do her necessary below-the-surface work. My Type-A personality often gets impatient and wants to make it happen now. I am continuing to learn this important lesson of natural timing.

> **My Type-A personality often gets impatient and wants to make it happen now. I am continuing to learn this important lesson of natural timing.**

Gay Lynn and I often marvel at how we didn't meet until the right time. We lived in the same city. I was on radio. She was on TV. We both interviewed people. She taught classes at my church. We attended some of the same lectures, shopped at the same health-food store. We both were single. We had very similar interests, spiritual searchings, vocations and mutual friends.

But right timing is a mysterious component of the life process that possesses its own wisdom. Gay Lynn and I both were praying, developing ourselves, and sometimes wondering why things didn't work out with people we were seeing. Later, we were thankful that those relationships didn't hatch into a marriage with someone else prematurely. We feel we are meant for each other. We had to be patient and wait for our right time and circumstance of meeting when we were ready. If either or both of us had married out of pressure, loneliness or convenience, and *then* we had met, the possibilities of our love and professional partnership probably would have been lost. You would never have seen the book you now hold in your hands.

I have treasured a poem by John Burroughs, a noted naturalist, who no doubt learned to patiently wait as he watched and worked with plants and animals. I have shared it with many people in spiritual counseling. It helps me calm myself and trust the Universe to bring forth the right and highest good in her own Divine timing and way.

## Waiting

Serene, I fold my hands and wait,
    Nor care for wind, or tide, or sea;
I rave no more 'gainst time or fate,
    For, lo! my own shall come to me.

I stay my haste, I made delays,
    For what avails this eager pace?
I stand amid the eternal ways,
    And what is mine shall know my face.

Asleep, awake, by night or day,
    The friends I seek are seeking me;
No wind can drive my bark astray,
    Nor change the tide of destiny.

What matter if I stand alone?
    I wait with joy the coming years;
My heart shall reap where it has sown,
    And garner up its fruit of tears.

The waters know their own and draw
    The brook that springs in yonder height;
So flows the good with equal law
    Unto the soul of pure delight.

The stars come nightly to the sky;
    The tidal wave unto the sea;
Nor time, nor space, nor deep, nor high,
    Can keep my own away from me.

JOHN BURROUGHS

I lovingly
serve life, and
life lovingly
blesses me
daily.

*Oakland, California*

# Charles Garfield: Peak Performer and Transformer

In 1974, David met Charles Garfield, the founder of the Shanti Project for cancer patients and their families and caregivers. Years later Charlie came to speak at Detroit Unity Temple. His accomplishments reveal his many talents. An Olympic champion weightlifter, Dr. Garfield was a psychologist with NASA and a professor at the University of California Medical School. He is best known for authoring *Peak Performance,* geared to athletes, and *Peak Performers,* targeted to business management. His most recent book, *Second to None,* deals with new paradigms for business that honor people and the Earth.

We met with Charlie at his home, high in the Oakland, California hills, where he lives with his wife, Cindy. We were privileged to experience a profound discussion, and share with you the wisdom of a great soul and teacher.

**Gay Lynn:** Describe the birth-giving process in your life.

**Charles:** For me it's always been about two things: What is viable for the self, and what is workable in the world. Viable to the self—deep self—means an expression of who

I am in a very basic way that meets an important need of my own that generalizes as a need for others and that is workable in the world.

You see people shooting themselves in the foot in a variety of ways. Some people are very fascinated with the deep psyche. They'll go into Jungian therapy and become experts on all matters Jungian, and be fascinated with their dream work. They don't *do* anything. They may or may not learn more about themselves, really. Hopefully they do. But, even if they do, they never take the next step, and maybe don't want to. I'm not judging. I'm simply saying they never take the next step, which is: "What does this say about the best use of my life in the world?"

**David:** They're over-read and underdone.

**Charles:** You have to move from internal to external frames of reference. Then you, as the Buddhists, take it into the marketplace to prove it works, like the hero's journey that [Joseph] Campbell made so popular. The bottom line is the hero goes back into the world. The hero goes through the dark night of the soul, takes the wisdom back and puts it to work.

**David:** Sometimes people may go to work at a place that is idealistically or spiritually oriented to be in that energy and soak it up. But that isn't enough. It doesn't get the job done. We're here to serve and help *and* we have to produce or we won't be able to stay in business.

**Charles:** Best expression of that I ever heard was from Steve Jobs when he was with Apple. He made the comment, "True artists ship." That is, true artists get their products out into the world. You have to be able to integrate the artist, the deep unconscious imagery and the information that comes from that imagery, with some expression in the world.

Let me give you a couple of examples that work really well for me. My career seems to be somewhat of a mystery to people. You may think I'm a corporate consultant, speaker,

> **Best expression of that I ever heard was from Steve Jobs when he was with Apple. He made the comment, "True artists ship."**

writer, which would be entirely reasonable. That's the Charlie Garfield many people know and identify with. I have to really hustle to identify with the guy who wrote these business books. I've had about six different careers, all of which have been very visible in the world and the Peak Performance business-writer/speaker/consultant was the last one. Now I'm right in the middle of the next career. There's much deeper reality that's been true regardless of *where* I've been out there.

**David:** You're aware of what you have done, and done well, but you are more than these accomplishments.

**Charles:** I grew up in a family where high achievement was just expected. It was just in the air. It was assumed. Now what's the link between that early influence and a guy who grows up to study and write books on peak perfor-mance?

**Gay Lynn:** The imprint was made early!

**Charles:** And made well. That is, it didn't have a lot of punitive overlay to it. I wasn't working out some early wound around being forced to excel. I knew early that you could do what you loved, and that was the single best way to begin a search for mission and expression of self. Trust the excitement! Trust this overwhelming feeling of loving what you're looking at. Don't launch until you have that feeling, because it's not going to work out. Take some steps. Find what excites you most. Then if you're real wise, and you have the time and inclination, try to find out what deeper psychological and spiritual influence is trying to be born here.

**Gay Lynn:** We're tapping into the excitement created as our masculine and feminine energies come together in us to birth new life for us.

**Charles:** You're right. There are many ways to describe these related energies in us. Jung, of course, called them *animus* and *anima*. We have separated these quite distinctly—calling one masculine and one feminine. And we've said even further that being very masculine is great and being very feminine is great. Being very masculine meant you'd better not have a whole lot of feminine. Being feminine meant you'd better not have a whole lot of masculine.

To see how we arrived at this strict separation in our society, you have to go back to power and dominance relations with male power over the feminine, not just over women, but over the feminine in themselves as men in power and control. The solution is the *integration* of masculine and feminine first and foremost in the psyche of human beings.

**Gay Lynn:** That's our strong belief, too.

**Charles:** I'm in the middle of some very interesting work now. I mentioned my new career shift. Right now I'm doing AIDS work. I'm working with AIDS caregivers and people with AIDS and finishing a book on this. I have close contact with the gay community in San Francisco. So I have a lot of friends in this community, and I've gotten to take a look at what it's like for people who have a different integration of masculine and feminine. I've seen the integration of these taking place in many different ways, ranging from a rejection of the opposite to an identification with the opposite, which isn't the solution either. I could say to you that I'm a woman, but there is plenty of evidence to suggest that isn't true. So I see gay guys looking for the same integrations I'm looking for, and coming at it from the opposite direction, in somewhat the same way women are trying to find that integration. I don't mean to represent all gay guys in a certain psychological role or pattern, which is most unfair. There are different positions in terms of integration of masculine and feminine, just as in straight men. Once in a while I run into someone who has really worked hard at this integration of feminine and masculine, and you see what a delight that integration can be. The person is comfortable with both the assertion side or master side, and communion side, the relationship side.

**David:** Are we making progress then in this integration?

**Charles:** I think for us to survive as a species—which is a phrase that everyone seems to use to say something ponderous, and I'm afraid I'm going to do the same thing—we're going to have to understand what this integration is about. To experience ourselves as connected to the Earth, as connected to the ecosystem, means we are going to have to move past a power and dominance patriarchal relationship to this planet Earth. We approach the Earth with an attitude: "I have power, mastery over you. I can use you for whatever

I want." As soon as you develop a more feminine attitude, you begin feeling yourself connected to all that is and lives.

> **We approach the Earth with an attitude: "I have power, mastery over you. I can use you for whatever I want." As soon as you develop a more feminine attitude, you begin feeling yourself connected to all that is and lives. You can't take out the rain forests and all these species any more than you could hit your spouse or your mother.**

You can't take out the rain forests and all these species any more than you could hit your spouse or your mother. It makes no sense. The integration of masculine and feminine principles is hand-in-glove, is basic, to our survival today. We are still trying to get control of things, which may have been necessary when we had unbelievable predators all over the place.

**David:** *Jurassic Park* for real.

**Charles:** Right. But now we're still talking about conquering space. Such an attitude is disastrous to our present and future living in a respectful relationship with our earth and universe.

**Gay Lynn:** You have been the guru of peak performance, teaching people to excel in sports and business. Now you're rallying us toward each other and the Earth. We believe that not only inner partnerships between our feminine and masculine natures are important, but also outer partnerships and co-creation between people. What has happened in your life to lead you in this new direction? How have relationships helped you?

**Charles:** Probably as much as anyone, short of celebrity folks, I'm associated with individual achievement more than anybody around. I never really felt comfortable with that, and then I finally realized I was promoting it. I knew something was wrong with it. I was proud of what I'd done, but there was something that wasn't getting said, and it kept grating. Then I realized what it was—that I had succumbed, like a lot of other people, to this peculiarly American (not only American, but it's definitely stronger in America) notion of the rugged individualist, the so-called self-made man. It's wonderful, it's great! I love it! Except any asset pushed too far becomes a liability. If you really do think you did it by yourself, you confuse source with conduit. I had to rethink a whole lot. I'm really seeing all the work on high achievement up to my book, *Second to None,* as Phase One. Phase Two is about collaboration, about interconnection. Phase Two is about integration of masculine and feminine internally and certainly in the world as well.

> **I'm really seeing all the work on high achievement up to my book, *Second to None,* as Phase One. Phase Two is about collaboration, about interconnection. Phase Two is about integration of masculine and feminine internally and certainly in the world as well.**

It's an opportune time to ask me about relationships in my own life. I have to ask myself a hard question—certainly very hard for the rugged individualist in me: "What would it take for relationships to be as important as personal mission?" Try that with a high-achieving individual some time! I mean, really answering, not just faking it, because all us silver-tongued devils are very good at talking.

**David:** We tell ourselves and our loved ones, "Of course, you are important. You know I would give the world for you. I always put people first."

**Charles:** Right!

**David:** But coaches, success motivators, sales-manager types, church growth consultants tell us: "You have to sacrifice to be a winner, to be Number One, to get to the top, to be world class. You can't let anything or anyone get in your way. You don't have time to waste, trying to meet other people's needs or agendas. Get them out of the way. Let it all go. And concentrate all your attention on your success and achievement. Go for it!"

**Charles:** Absolutely! And what are the consequences of that message? Relationships are secondary. Relationship with yourself is secondary. Relationship with anything out of your bailiwick of mission-driven activity doesn't really matter. Tunnel vision.

> Clearly, interconnectedness is what everybody's talking about when they talk about a "living systems model."
>
> There is a living systems model and a machine model of the universe. If the universe works like a machine, what does that make me? A machine part.

I'm very proud of what I've done, and people who have done great work in the world should be proud of what they do. People who have done great work in their own life should be proud. But the model of personal achievement is too narrow. What's a bigger paradigm that can hold individual accomplishment and achievement but that acknowledges the interconnectedness of us all?

Clearly, interconnectedness is what everybody's talking about when they talk about a "living systems model." There is a living systems model and a machine model of the universe. If the universe works like a machine, what does that make me? A machine part. So I'm trying to be the best machine part I can be. Which is pretty much the way high achievers like me act. Goals, plans, corrections. Fit in. Get in gear. Full speed ahead. Crank it out. Readjust. Recalibrate. Blueprints for success. Numbers. Scoreboards. Ratings. Compute. Count.

**David:** And we are driven or get driven by others or the mechanistic system we get enmeshed in.

**Charles:** So now I'm looking at the question you ask about relationship in life: How does one learn what one needs to learn if the essential learning is about collaboration, interdependency in relationships?

**David:** Where do we learn this?

**Charles:** The very first thing is to access internally what that's about. If I went out and decided, now I'm a relationship person, I'll just make a plan—that makes no sense. You can't get there from here. I have to access a collaborative sensibility with my deep self. My first relationship is with me, internally. Who is this man? Do I like him? Do I not like aspects of him?

This exploration of myself has been fascinating. I'm making it sound like it all came after the realization of working on individual high achievement. Finding that achievement is necessary but not sufficient. But in fact a whole lot of it went on all along, I just didn't see inner and outer relationships as central.

The Shanti Project, which did cancer work and turned out to be the first AIDS caregiving organization in the whole country, was all about relationships. I find myself more proud of that than anything I ever did. When I go back in my life to the times I was most gratified and happiest, I ask myself, what about it made me feel so good? Many of those occasions admittedly were about achievement, but the imagery was all about celebrating with somebody else. Or thinking about its impact on people. I never once had an image of myself making a killing in the stock market because of smart investment and ending up loaded with money. I never even had the image of a gold medalist on a stand, although I've had my share of that kind of experience. I always wanted to get off the stand and bring the trophy to somebody to talk about it. And then I was going to show them that they could do that same thing. It was this teacher function that was always trying to get born when I was competing as a weightlifter.

**David:** The peak is not just something to be attained by you or me now, but found together and shared.

**Charles:** Now that the search for collaboration, the feminine dimension—call it the communion aspect—has moved to center stage, I find myself involved in several circles. One I do each Thursday night with AIDS caregivers, where I find some of the most stunning stuff that I've ever experienced in my life. We take people who are around life and death issues all the time. We pull back for an evening a week and say, "What's going on with you?" Whew! The stuff that's shared is unbelievable. "What's the best use of my life in the time I have?" "Who am I really?" All kinds of existential and spiritual views and searchings that are basic to these life-and-death situations.

**David:** Your life has turned in quite a different direction. I remember you hurrying off the plane from Washington, D.C., to Detroit to speak one evening. You were on a fast track in the 1980s.

**Charles:** I used to have a speaking schedule that would have killed a horse—120 speeches a year for 12 years. Plus I consulted with companies and taught at the University of California Medical School. [Stephen] Covey and I started the newsletter Executive Excellence in the early 1980s. I was out there generating, speaking, doing. Now I'm here in this beautiful place. I spend all of my time with my wife, Cindy, and our friends. Somebody said to me recently, "Charlie, it looks like you've retired!" "No," a friend responded, "he's living the contemplative life." I'll buy that. I don't know how contemplative it is. What makes me feel good now—just as the speaking did then—is being close to people in small-scale human groupings. Call it circles, call it one-on-one—where the emotions are not those of triumph but of communion.

**David:** That's quite a transformation.

**Charles:** There's clearly a transformative element to all of us. But I see it as transformative in the sense that what's going on for me personally is the development of previously underdeveloped aspects. They were real the whole time. The guy who founded Shanti Project so that people could take care of other people is hardly the world's most typical rugged individualist. That guy who is very good at orchestrating noteworthy achievements that other people, as well as himself, find admirable—he's still alive, and I can access that guy pretty fast. But now he's in the service of something else, something that is much more—what one could call feminine/community.

**Gay Lynn:** What is that community?

**Charles:** Community for me means deep soul connection with other people and all that lives.

**Gay Lynn:** Do you sense there's a profound loneliness among people?

**Charles:** Ah! It's tragic. We are essentially nomads. We are tribes of one. We are niche markets of one. Alone in the world, we pretend to have relationships. And when we have one that has any depth, we call it a peak experience because we don't know that it's normal.

> **Ah! It's tragic. We are essentially nomads. We are tribes of one. We are niche markets of one. Alone in the world, we pretend to have relationships. And when we have one that has any depth, we call it a peak experience because we don't know that it's normal.**

**David:** Jung said that the second half of life is not lived the same as the first half. Often it's more interior, contemplative, soulful, valuing communion rather than conquest.

**Charles:** I was always aware of internal origins, though. A lot of the achievers that I met and studied didn't sense there was any internal origin to what they chose at all. They thought it was all chosen by what is workable in the world. I knew I couldn't do anything unless I loved it deeply. I knew I'd be helpless if I tried to launch something because it was practical. I don't think I'm overdramatizing this by saying I'm virtually incapable of following something unless there's great excitement there. Other people seem to be able to turn themselves into machines in order to crank it out.

**Gay Lynn:** Life was always lived from the inside out for you?

**Charles:** I was always aware of an internal locus, of deeper needs being met. I went through a strong period around the Bay area in my 20s and 30s when this area was so attuned to spiritual matters, and so was I.

Jung's statement is one about the evolution of the deep psyche. I think he can get misinterpreted in the sense that, first you do this, then you do that. I think it's balance. All along you're doing both. The "in-the-world achievement mode" is more prominent earlier; it's not that the spiritual searching comes later. The background can become the foreground in mid-life and beyond. Once you are aware of what the forces are, you have a choice. It's easy to say, "I'm going to let go of the high achievement, goal-setting, higher performance in the outer life and let myself be with relationships, communion, sharing life." But try it some-time, especially for a man in our society!

**Gay Lynn:** What are some steps to help in making this new birth?

**Charles:** Recognize that some of the times in your past where you have been most sublimely happy have precisely been moments when you shared yourself and connected significantly. You are not starting from scratch. You've had experiences historically that were manifestations of the fem-inine dimension. Don't be afraid of that word "feminine," what you believe it connotes about weakness, about being one-down, about being not quite a man. The feminine aspect of yourself, when developed, will allow you much greater fulfillment than you have ever had before, even in your finest individual achievements. Don't think that it means abandoning your ability to be viable in the world. It may mean you will choose different arenas in which to express yourself and different ways to express.

**David:** I saw a man the other day with a company T-shirt that said, "Working Together Works."

**Charles:** Understand, that may be the deepest level, to allow for the emergence of the feminine part of ourselves, to allow for a communion with others and all that lives. And that communion is the way the world really works best. To align with that principle is to harmonize with the way things really are. If we make it, we'll survive and flourish because you and others like you work together.

**David:** Life *is* synergistic—a synthesis of energies.

**Charles:** Yes! Life is synergistic. To pretend that life is individualistic and compartmentalized is suicidal. You can't go up to a rosebud, pull all the petals off, and say, "Bloom, dammit, I don't have time to wait around!" It has its own internal logic because it is part of an ecosystem.

> **Life *is* synergistic. To pretend that life is individualistic and compartmentalized is suicidal. You can't go up to a rosebud, pull all the petals off, and say, "Bloom, dammit, I don't have time to wait around!" It has its own internal logic because it is part of an ecosystem.**

**David:** We are part of a Divine Order. That miracle of growth and birthing is described in Aesop's fable of "The Goose That Laid the Golden Eggs." What does this fable say to you?

**Charles:** It's a parable for our time. It's what's going on in the rain forests. It's the approach of many corporations. It's assertion in the world run amok. It's seeing only in cause-and-effect fashion and not seeing that a larger context applies. What are the implications of your actions more contextually? What happens when we act unilaterally rather than collaboratively?

Perhaps we need to establish a relationship with the Goose, attain Goose-consciousness, to learn what was going on. It was an organic process, not a machine process. [The greedy man] thought there was gold on the inside and the Goose was a delivery machine which made it oval. But if you think from a more organic, living systems model, then you might understand gestation, evolution and the right timing of things.

You can feel sorry for the greedy man because he sees himself as opposed to all else. There's him and there's all else. He's trying to win. He doesn't understand that he is intimately connected to that which he is competing with. He doesn't get it. He kills what could sustain him and enrich him and do good for many people.

**Gay Lynn:** How can we get this relationship to the organic process that we're part of which births golden eggs in our lives?

**Charles:** It will be common sense when a new consciousness is born. It will be the new common sense. We won't have to ask, "How do we go get it?" The question is, "How do human beings experience themselves as interconnected?" Here's where we have to do our own individual work. I'm trying to do it myself.

Read the wisdom literature, not just the esoteric and mystical works. It's there. Read the words of wise people. "The formula for despair is to live a life that has no service to others." Go back in your life to a time when you were most gratified. I suspect you are looking at a context that involved interdependency in relationship.

It all has to do with the evolving human consciousness, with an allowance for aspects of yourself that formerly were seen as subservient. Let those aspects move to the fore and come to fruition. Allow the feminine to emerge more fully, to take center stage.

**David:** Do we put the same commitment, time, money, effort, goal-setting into developing this contextual life as we put into—or used to put into—the get-ahead, self-interest, "winning" way of life?

**Charles:** Most people take workshops. They read a book. But it's like trying to push a battleship. It requires a different level of commitment. It requires the same level as you made to a more assertive, achievement strategy, to the old paradigm. I have a lot of respect for the enormity of the task, because we're really talking about an evolutionary task that's multigenerational. There is an emergency involved here, and it's necessary we do this task as quickly as possible.

**David:** It's a crisis/opportunity.

**Charles:** One last thing: In working with lots of dying people, one of the things you see is people evolving more rapidly because of the catastrophic consequences of what they are facing. It's very dramatic with children who have life-threatening illnesses. They become little adults. Also, we're amazed at the wisdom of 20- and 30-year-olds dying of AIDS. We often just ask, "With all this going on in your life, how does the world look to you now?" Talk about some of the best teachers I ever had! They've made the shift because of catastrophe.

So, because of global danger and catastrophe, we have to make the shift. And not only because of catastrophic implications, but because of its "benestrophic" rewards. Everyone knows the negative, but what are the beneficial consequences of shifting to valuing ourselves, people and the earth?

> **So, because of global danger and catastrophe, we have to make the shift. And not only because of catastrophic implications, but because of its "benestrophic" rewards.**

It's folks like you trying to articulate it for us. Hold up pictures. Tell me parables. Make movies. Write poems. The more we do collectively, the more we align behind a coherent vision. The more we are likely to demonstrate it.

It's going to happen through stories. When the stories we tell each other are stories of communion, collaboration and connection, and those stories become the new common sense, then we'll be on the road.

# On Work

*But I say to you that when you work you fulfill a part of earth's furthest dream, assigned to you when that dream was born,*

*And in keeping yourself with labour you are in truth loving life,*

*And to love life through labour is to be intimate with life's inmost secret.*

THE PROPHET
BY *KAHLIL GIBRAN*

# 5

# Discovering the Soul in Relationships

# Thoughts from David:
## Discovering the Soul in Relationships

A traditional interpretation of the Adam and Eve story in Genesis has Eve being a helper to Adam (Genesis 18: "I will make him a helper as his partner.") Conservative, patriarchal Christian wedding services often designate the husband as the head of the marriage and the wife as his helper or servant. The ritual of the father giving away his daughter to the new master of the house acts out this servant/property relationship. The daughter-servant now is given over to a new master as wife-servant.

When we officiate at weddings, we interpret the helping relationships in a totally different way. Both husband and wife are helpers to each other. Each aids and supports the other in finding and giving greater expression to their innate divinity. This is one reason why they have been attracted to each other—to learn and grow together in spiritual maturity, giving their best to each other and the world.

Over the years in thousands of marriages and couple counseling sessions, we have seen what is commonly referred to as a "soul attraction." A soul attraction is an affinity one feels toward another person beyond a mutual sharing of common interests. It extends to a core level of wanting to experience some soul lessons with this person.

> **So many times the little things about the partner that bother us the most are the very characteristics we may be lacking or perhaps also have a need to overcome. We project that quality or problem onto the other person, simultaneously desiring it or being bugged by it in him or her. Our partner mirrors our own soul.**

Often we have observed that the soul is in some need of balance within itself, and seeks out the relationship as a means to fulfill this balance. Finding inner balance by having a love relationship with this other person can be both an exciting and challenging experience.

So many times the little things about the partner that bother us the most are the very characteristics we may be lacking or perhaps also have a need to overcome. We project that quality or problem onto the other person, simultaneously desiring it or being bugged by it in him or her. Our partner mirrors our own soul.

The most endearing qualities are our attempt to embrace the Divine in ourselves. Our soul is attracted to or desires a quality or ability that our loved one has. But often we may resist that very trait to which we are drawn and it may eventually annoy us.

One man was once attracted to a free-spirited woman because he wasn't that way. He needed to lighten up his intensity and be freer in his life, to play and be more spontaneous. The quality he enjoyed most in the beginning caused the relationship's demise because ultimately it bugged him that she never could really engage in life in a practical and meaningful way. His soul learned what it needed from the relationship; he was much freer and fun to be with. The relationship had come to teach him a valuable soul lesson.

Not all soul partnerships are lifelong relationships. People may enter our lives and then move on to prepare us for our real soul partner, which may result in a longer, more balanced and committed relationship. In all our relationships we need to ask ourselves, "What soul and life lessons has this person come to teach me? What qualities or characteristics am I most attracted to? Are these qualities or characteristics that I need to develop to enhance my own life?"

We pose this question to couples in prewedding counseling: "Why do you think you are getting married?" People usually respond by saying, somewhat indignantly at times, "Because we love each other!" A deeper soul-searching needs to take place in ongoing friendships as the highs and lows of relating occur.

We affirm in the wedding ceremony, "May you continue to communicate as directly and honestly as you can with each other—sharing with the purpose of increasing understanding and growing through situations. Don't just let your relationship deteriorate into small talk and outer concerns. Speak to each other of your inner feelings, needs, values, goals and the desires of your hearts. May you have a soul relationship always. Listen to each other. Let each other know what is happening in a way so that the other can help or try to understand." We help each other to unite the Divine Feminine and Masculine energies within ourselves to give birth to our God love and potential.

I was the senior minister of a large church in the middle of Detroit when I met Gay Lynn in 1985. Our marriage vows, affirmed before hundreds—our family, friends and congregation—included a commitment to serve God and our spiritual community. Gay Lynn worked for years with me in the church—supporting, assisting, mending fences, leading, studying, teaching, praying, counseling, visiting, planning, coordinating, writing, networking to help me fulfill my calling in ministry. She helped birth our ministry to thousands of people each week.

In that same spirit of cooperation and commitment, I assumed responsibility for almost all work and home activities while Gay Lynn earned her master's degree in Clinical and Humanistic Psychology. I knew the value of earning the degree and felt the excitement of her expanded growth as she took on that educational challenge. Enlarging her educational horizon stimulated a new level of sharing and depth in our relationship. We experienced the joy of discussing new topics and making new friendships. Expanding the scope of learning for Gay Lynn kept our relationship fresh and alive. I was secure enough in myself to enthusiastically encourage Gay Lynn in fulfilling one of her life goals, while not feeling abandoned or left out in the process.

After completing her master's degree at the Center for Humanistic Studies in Detroit, Michigan, and writing her thesis on ritual and transformation, it came to Gay Lynn to begin authoring our first book. She was facilitating the special ceremony done on the first Sunday of the New Year, called the White Stone Ceremony. The ceremony entails using a piece of white, unglazed tile stone to fulfill the Biblical passage in Revelation 2:17 and receive a new name on the clean slate for a new life experience.

Two words were written on Gay Lynn's white stone— "Published Author"—as a revelation to be fulfilled. That message clearly beckoned her to take a particular course of action. Gay Lynn was not exactly aware of what that meant or how to go about fulfilling that life work, so she started meditating and writing. I supported her, wrote with her, became her editor, and co-presented with her to a good publisher which accepted the book for publication. I helped Gay Lynn give birth to that which called to her. Developed in love, the book was born into the world as the first of many offspring. This project opened our life-work to serve and reach out to thousands of people, touching lives around the world.

> **I helped Gay Lynn give birth to that which called to her. Developed in love, the book was born into the world as the first of many offspring. This project opened our life-work to serve and reach out to thousands of people touching lives around the world.**

## Helping One Another Give Birth

Let these questions be an opening to us all as we cooperate consciously with the birthing process. Answer them for yourself and share them with your partner.

What is life calling me to give birth to?
What wants to grow in me and spring forth?

What gifts of God in me are to be born out into the world? How can I let this Divine birthing take place?

How can my partner, family, friends and co-workers help as spiritual midwives or mid-husbands to support me with my delivery?

How can I help my partner, children, parents, friends, co-workers, colleagues, associates, students, congregation, patients, clients, customers, neighbors, community and humanity give birth to their golden eggs or treasures?

## Multiple Births?

Look for ways to honor and enthusiastically support one another. Sometimes the focus of support may be more on one partner than another. Let this be agreed upon as a process of life, each giving birth in his own way or in her own timing. Some births may be simultaneous, like having twins.

> **The mothering instinct in us all sometimes fantasizes about taking care of all the new babies and nourishing all their needs. This misconception can end up leaving us drained physically, stressed-out emotionally, and may have severe repercussions on our familial relationships.**

Remember the extra care and energy required to take care of more than one birth at a time. Your life can become consumed with such projects. Are you both giving birth? Are you sharing a birth? Are you having multiple births?

Multiple births require a concentrated amount of extra energy. One baby may be peacefully sleeping while the other is crying to be fed. In such a scenario, there is little time for rest and recreation time for the parents. Many births may come to us, wanting our time and attention. The mothering instinct in us all sometimes fantasizes about taking care of all the new babies and nourishing all their needs. This misconception can end up leaving us drained physically, stressed-out emotionally, and may have severe repercussions on our familial relationships. Be clear and selective as to what you commit to giving birth to. Let the pregnancies be planned as much as possible, or at least make an adequate amount of time and vitality available to really give your births the best chance for viability.

When a new birth is welcomed and lovingly supported by the family and community around it, its chances of flourishing are greatest. Let us be helpmates to one another as we are in union and in Divine love each day.

Don't
push and don't
hold back—
what's the next
step? What's the
next step?

*Sausalito, California*

# The Magnetic and Dynamic Angeles Arrien

Angeles Arrien is a cultural anthropologist and a renowned speaker and author who has done her research work on the four universal addictive behaviors. She has demonstrated through her work that change can be handled creatively by working with eight universal beliefs that sustain health and well-being in all cultures. We talked to Angeles about the Divine Feminine and Divine Masculine and how they operate in our lives.

Angeles' houseboat is nestled in a lovely little harbor, surrounded by the beautiful bay across from San Francisco. We relaxed by the lovely old stove in the cozy living room, peering out onto the sunny bay waters.

**Gay Lynn:** What does the Divine Feminine look like? How does it operate in our lives, and how would you describe our relationship to that part of ourselves?

**Angeles:** I like to think of the Divine Feminine as the magnetic force in each human being, be they male or female. The force of magnetism is the capacity to hold, draw forth, open, receive, and deepen our life experience. We need to

**Angeles Arrien**

be conscious about what we draw toward us, what we open ourselves to, and ask ourselves: How open and receptive are we to life? Magnetism is the force within us that requires that we integrate and deepen our experience.

It is not a gender type; it is a universal experience, a human experience. Spirituality is a human experience. With the male and female we deal with two forces: magnetism, which I just described, and dynamism, which is the opposite.

Dynamism is the capacity to expand, create, bring things into manifestation. Women who give physical birth are experiencing the dynamic energy. Birth is not a receptive process—the insemination is receptive, but the actual birthing process is dynamic. Dynamic energy is required to bring things into form, whereas the capacity to deepen and the capacity to integrate are definitely magnetic energy.

> **I like to think of the Divine Feminine as the magnetic force in each human being, be they male or female. The force of magnetism is the capacity to hold, draw forth, open, receive, and deepen our life experience. We need to be conscious about what we draw toward us, what we open ourselves to, and ask ourselves: How open and receptive are we to life?**

So I can't deepen or integrate anything until I slow down, and open and receive the experience, person or situation. I feel that being conscious about the feminine energy within is to be aware of what needs to be integrated, deepened, and synthesized within my nature.

I would rather put it in terms of magnetic and dynamic because these are not gender issues. I feel it is a spiritual issue. We are the only culture to make the separation as strongly as we do between the masculine and feminine. The magnetic and dynamic forces are spiritual, transformative energies.

> **I would rather put it in terms of magnetic and dynamic because these are not gender issues. I feel it is a spiritual issue. We are the only culture to make the separation as strongly as we do between the masculine and feminine. The magnetic and dynamic forces are spiritual, transformative energies.**

**David:** We tend to talk about it or assign to it "masculine" or "feminine . . ."

**Angeles:** Which is a very logos thing to do. It is not an eros thing to do, to assign it, which then uses our dynamic function. Logos is our wisdom nature to objectify things or put things in categories. Eros is magnetic energy and much more embracing and synthesizing. So from a cross-cultural point of view, certain things are literally seen as dynamic and magnetic. They can be put in four categories:

## Dynamic Energies:

1. Words, and possibly communicating well, draws from dynamism, requires you to go out and speak.
2. Leadership demands that you show up; that's dynamism.
3. The ability to produce or manifest is dynamic energy.
4. The capacity to assign meaning or significance is dynamic energy.

## Magnetic Energies:

1. Paying attention to ritual, ceremony or tradition is magnetic.
2. Trusting our vision, insight and intuition is magnetic.

3. Our capacity to organize and systematize things is magnetic.
4. Our ability to nurture and feel is magnetic.

Men and women who have a good identification with all eight of these things are considered balanced. And so our journey is a balanced one.

I think ascribing gender words to universal processes is something that lends to the confusion and to the separation. These universal processes are part of the spiritual experience that both men and women in their life need to address.

What was popularly called the feminist movement was really a large number of women claiming their dynamic energy, sometimes at the expense and sacrifice of the magnetic, feminine energy. I think the masculine movement, the men's movement, may be the same—claiming of the magnetic at the expense of the dynamic aspects. Both are required in each of us as part of our spiritual unfolding.

> **What was popularly called the feminist movement was really a large number of women claiming their dynamic energy, sometimes at the expense and sacrifice of the magnetic, feminine energy. I think the masculine movement, the men's movement, may be the same—claiming of the magnetic at the expense of the dynamic aspects. Both are required in each of us as part of our spiritual unfolding.**

**Gay Lynn:** We shared with you Aesop's fable of "The Goose That Laid the Golden Eggs." How do you see that story relating to our own spiritual birthing process?

**Angeles:** I think it is a story of the beauty of magnetic energy, which is the ability to honor the right timing and the cycles of things. There is a part in us and in nature that knows how to wait and gestate and honor the timing of giving birth. And then, whether we are male or female, there are also parts of us that are impatient, greedy, and will push or hold back the process as represented by the farmer.

The birthing process is a universal process internally and externally. It is experienced in the female body. It is also experienced internally in both men and women. Externally in the man, the birthing process is the capacity to bring things into form, in projects and expressions of creativity. And the same thing is true for women, only a woman gives biological birth, which requires that she go into the dynamic energy. It is her initiation. Every woman that gives birth has her initiation into the creative fire, into the masculine energy.

So I see "The Goose That Laid the Golden Eggs" as the story of the magnetic energy, the forces of birthing, both the negative force—being expedient and greedy—and the one that honors organic cycles. These are the two forces of birthing. Sometimes we will abort things, become expedient and greedy. Sometimes we continue to honor the organic cycle, the right timing, the next phase or stage of a project, or a relationship, or a baby's development.

**Gay Lynn:** You have birthed many things. What was the birthing process like as you were engaged in it?

**Angeles:** Each birth has been different, totally different! It's had its own timing—moving in a faster rhythm, slower rhythm, medium rhythm. Each has had its own complications and challenges.

**Gay Lynn:** Partnerships are a vital part of the birthing process. Describe that loving and supportive system that helps us to deliver.

**Angeles:** I think there are three ways in which we birth:
1. We birth alone.
2. We birth with a significant partner, friend or colleague.
3. We birth in teams, collectives or communities.

These are the three universal processes in which we live, move and have our life unfold every day. Each of these can relate to a different kind of birthing experience. I have birthed alone, I have birthed with a partner and in a group.

**Gay Lynn:** Birthing alone, what is that like for you?

**Angeles:** In my training program we do three days and two nights in solitude. Also, I have a personal practice of one day per month being in the silence, listening to the guidance that is within me. I know there has never been a project that I have been involved with that I didn't have to spend time with alone. That alone

> **I have a personal practice of one day per month being in the silence, listening to the guidance that is within me.**

time is what I call the "sacred time." It's doing my alone time in the birthing process.

With a partner we learn about collaboration. With a team, we are learning about group skills and community building. And they all involve a different commitment to what we are creating.

**David:** Companionship with nature is also important to you?

**Angeles:** Outer nature is a mirror for one's internal nature.

I need to spend time in nature every day. I feel that's where the gestation, the reflection, the mirroring occurs. The degree to which people can be connected to outer nature is the degree to which people can be connected to their inner nature. And the degree to which people are separated from outer nature is the degree to which they are separated from their inner nature.

**David:** How do you connect with nature?

**Angeles:** I go out on the deck of the houseboat or walk the trails. I make time for a walk every day, even when I am traveling and speaking.

**Gay Lynn:** In the process of birth there are always birthing pains, challenges. How do you get through those times?

**Angeles:** I think the golden goose story is a good example of what happens when we won't stay with the natural labor and the natural timing. We end up sacrificing what is attempting to come through by our own impatience. The ego needs to control the outcome, rather than to let it come and take the next step. The next step may be staying flexible, following what has more heart meaning for me, pursuing the integrity, staying in touch with that energy, and seeing how I can have fun with this and maintain a sense of humor.

> I think the golden goose story is a good example of what happens when we won't stay with the natural labor and the natural timing. We end up sacrificing what is attempting to come through by our own impatience.

There are always challenges in the creative process.

Each challenge is different with each project, and I know there will be a boulder in my path somewhere.

**Gay Lynn:** How do you get around the boulders in life?

**Angeles:** You explore the boulder, creatively problem-solve. Within the birthing process is a creative process. I see the boulders as a creative problem-solving opportunity. This is where the boulder is and it's stuck, and I check out if I am stuck, or am I pushing?

**Gay Lynn:** We can ask ourselves, where am I with this problem? Am I stuck or am I pushing?

**Angeles:** Yes, and I use a mantra for myself: "Don't push and don't hold back. What's the next step? What's the next step?"

**Gay Lynn:** That's a wonderful mantra for birthing our lives.

**David:** How do other cultures deal with the masculine and feminine dichotomy in a less dualistic sort of way?

**Angeles:** In the majority of land-based or indigenous cultures, the roles are clearly defined and respected. The kitchen is a sacred domain, whoever is in it, man or woman. Tending the crops is a sacred stewardship, and depending on when extra help is needed in either place, men and women work together. There is a difference between roles being clearly defined and people being suppressed. Where roles are clearly defined, we find respect. I don't feel that the roles were clearly defined in the pioneering days, and I think that is happening now with the computer superhighway. The Internet is another pioneering frontier, a massive, collective birthing taking place. People look to one another as creative resources rather than

> **People look to one another as creative resources rather than "You're a man, so you do this," and "I am a woman, so I do that."**

"You're a man, so you do this," and "I am a woman, so I do that."

The real danger as we move into the 21st century is that we are put into the gender blender rather than being regarded as human beings with certain skills, talents and abilities, and we use them together to birth the next creative process.

**Gay Lynn:** How do we birth our global community and world soul together? What is your vision for that process?

**Angeles:** I feel that will occur in a step-by-step process as people begin to bring an awareness into their own family of their internal nature.

**Gay Lynn:** How could families do this?

**Angeles:** I think mothers and fathers can do this by acknowledging and supporting their children's creative endeavors. Creating is beautiful and precious and wonderful. It doesn't have any judgments on it at all. The child is like "The Goose That Laid the Golden Eggs" and the parents might sometimes be like the farmer—wanting the child to do something in their timing, and their way, not in the child's timing and way. I think we need to look at our children as the goose with the golden eggs. They are our resources for the future.

**Gay Lynn:** The children have the golden eggs?

**Angeles:** They do, and we have to help facilitate the organic part of the process. The greatest impact that we can ever make is on a child, to give our creative support to a child on a consistent basis. The mystery that every parent experiences with every child is the mystery that we experience as we go to a global village. In the global village we creatively support Mother Nature, the Gaia consciousness, which also has the golden eggs. It is a new age of partnership with the planet. Without pushing the planet, or trying to be expedient about it, we are working with the organic creative process.

**Gay Lynn:** People are anxious about the violence, death, destruction and disasters they see on the TV and in the newspaper.

**Angeles:** We are going through the birthing process. Birth is very bloody, birth isn't pretty; it's very, very messy.

**David:** And there can be a lot of screaming and rushing around.

**Angeles:** Oh yes, we are in an intense labor process. Labor is not easy.

**David:** What about those who fear the labor process and panic because of all the changes taking place?

**Angeles:** I don't know, because I don't feel I am supposed to steer other people's processes, other than to provide comfort along the journey, or wisdom to lessen the fear. I can offer love to temper their fear. Fear is a human experience. That's why we teach people to manage their fear. Love is stronger than fear. So I think we need to be more loving, to call to our loving nature, rather than to fight fear with fear.

There is no easy answer. It is part of the mystery. Like

birth is part of the mystery, death is a mystery, marriage is a mystery, initiation is a mystery. Our task is to be like the hollow little bones and let the mystery fill us instead of trying to control it.

I love what the Appalachian people say: "What's learnin' ya?" "What's workin' ya?" Pay attention to what is learnin' ya and workin' ya.

**Gay Lynn:** You mentioned significant times in our lives of birth, death, marriage and initiations. These are all rites of passage that take place on an inner and outer level.

**Angeles:** That's right, because all births are ritualized in every culture. All marriages, all initiations, all deaths are ritualized. And so we recognize that we use ritual to support change. And we use ritual to support that which we do not fully understand.

**Gay Lynn:** How does the ritual help us to enter the mystery?

**Angeles:** The setting up of ritual is a conscious intention to do ceremony for sacred purposes.

**David:** And to mark that change . . .

**Angeles:** It marks that change and it is witnessed by the community.

**David:** It goes beyond the mental realm. So much of metaphysics was holding the thought in our minds. Ritual goes beyond that and is holistic—mind, body and spirit—and is acted out in ceremony.

**Gay Lynn:** Our spirituality and our sexuality run the same pathway in the chakra system, although we tend to separate the body and our sexuality from the mind and spirit.

**Angeles:** Yes, we separate them into the sacred and the profane. That's why I think we are merging into a "both/and" world. We can no longer afford to put things into either/or and sacred or profane. Going into the 21st century will be a weaving of the both/and consciousness. The separations won't work; they become much more painful. The body is the spirit, and the spirit is in the body.

We learn that we have no immunity to the mystery, and we have no immunity to our body and ultimately to our death, so it is about befriending. Being comfortable in both the inner world and the outer world. We can't just stay in the outer world and not go in, and we can't stay in the inner world and never go out. Somewhere we have to bring one into the other and befriend them both. That's what I call walking the spiritual path with practical feet. That's the secret!

"Spirit hands
are on my head.
Father, Mother
blessing me. Comfort
courses down like
rain, cleansing and
caressing me."

—*Carol Lynn Pearson*

*Walnut Creek, California*

# Carol Lynn Pearson:
# Mother Wove the Morning

Carol Lynn Pearson was first a performer, then a writer. Now, with her one-woman play, *Mother Wove the Morning,* she combines those two gifts in what she feels is the most important work of her professional life.

Carol Lynn is the author of five books of poetry, which to date have sold over 250,000 copies. Her most recent works are *Women I Have Known and Been* and *Picture Window.* Ms. Pearson received her B.A. and M.A. in drama at Brigham Young University, and is a dedicated, lifelong member of the Mormon church.

Her autobiography, *Goodbye, I Love You,* tells the story of life with her husband Gerald, the struggle his homosexuality brought to their marriage, their divorce, and his subsequent death from AIDS in Carol Lynn's home, where she cared for him.

Carol Lynn has worked and lived in Walnut Creek, California with her four children since 1976. We sat in her sitting-room/study/bedroom surrounded by beautiful wall-paper displaying blooming roses. Carol Lynn says she finds the vitality of the flowered walls to be life-affirming. On the

**Carol Lynn Pearson**

bottom half of the wall beneath the chair rail are bold navy blue, wine and green stripes, which provide her a good masculine base, she says.

**Gay Lynn:** Could you describe your image of God as you were growing up?

**Carol Lynn:** I grew up in an anthropomorphic religion where God was a Divine, perfected male. We were taught that we have the potential of becoming as God. This is a very clear teaching in my religion. Along with that, although not as developed, is the concept of God as Mother, so that there is the Divine couple. All Mormons know "Our Heavenly Mother," and yet they would say, "Oh, yes, and we will know more about the Mother sometime."

**Gay Lynn:** How do you visualize this for yourself?

**Carol Lynn:** In my own mind, I am comfortable visualizing a perfect female, a magnificent being, bigger than life, yet still identifiable enough as Mother in a way that is more anthropomorphic.

I do not choose to just focus on her to the exclusion of the masculine because I feel I want balance, I want both. So as I do any visualizations or, often when I pray, I envision a perfect Divine couple with their hands on my head, giving me a blessing. And I can also envision myself being in the arms of the Divine Mother.

> I do not choose to just focus on her to the exclusion of the masculine because I feel I want balance, I want both. So as I do any visualizations or, often when I pray, I envision a perfect Divine couple with their hands on my head, giving me a blessing. And I can also envision myself being in the arms of the Divine Mother.

**David:** What does the greedy behavior of the man in the "Goose That Laid the Golden Eggs" represent to you?

**Carol Lynn:** The man's behavior represents the worst of patriarchal culture, wanting to dominate, not revering what happens to be there. In a spirit of greed the man has put himself higher than anybody else or the process of nature. Then he violently makes that happen for his own immediate, short-term benefit.

**Gay Lynn:** You have birthed many things in your life, along with four wonderful children. Can you describe the birthing process when you are writing?

**Carol Lynn:** Well, I can sometimes pinpoint a conception! I know when something has done a little click in my brain, that says "Ahhh, this is a possibility for the real project."

*Mother Wove the Morning,* with 16 women from prehistory to the present speaking about their lives, came with me from wherever I came from in the other world before I arrived here. I came here with something of a feminist consciousness.

In high school, long before Betty Friedan did her thing, I was saying, "What's wrong with this picture?" I grew up in Utah as a Mormon, and I was treated with a lot of kindness and given a lot of opportunity. Yet there was clearly something missing. In my femaleness, I was somewhere out on the fringe, and maleness was in the center. And something in me—not from my ego—said this was wrong.

*Mother Wove the Morning* kept coming to me, wanting my attention, finally screaming at me, until I said okay, and gave it my attention and energy. It then just fell into place as this play, and it required a lot of work to make it happen.

Other projects just say, "Ahhh," in the beginning, and I take the time and thought to let it develop. Then I can pretty much know when it is birthed.

**Gay Lynn:** Nurturing partnerships, friendships and communities of supportive people are so important when we are birthing our creations. Can you describe how you are nourished and supported in this way?

**Carol Lynn:** I had a very odd partnership with my husband that was helpful and painful at the same time.

As a human being, he was very supportive, very excited with the ideas I was working with. He borrowed $2,000 to publish my first book of poems. He was enormously helpful and supportive.

> **We found ourselves in this bizarre position. He was a homosexual, and his homosexuality profoundly negated my femaleness. Certainly my church, seemingly God, and now my husband all prefer men! It's hard to negate femaleness on any more levels than these.**

We found ourselves in this bizarre position. He was a homosexual, and his homosexuality profoundly negated my femaleness. Certainly my church, seemingly God, and now my husband all prefer men! It's hard to negate femaleness on any more levels than these.

So, in spite of that and because of that, I think, life thrusts us into the fire—the pressure cooker—to insist that the thing we came here to do gets going as fast as possible.

I am okay with the fact that I have been put in a marriage to a homosexual man, and in a very deep relationship to a patriarchal church. That challenged me on all fronts. I had to either die psychically and spiritually or scream out loud that femaleness is of equal value and has got to be honored and listened to and revered, which I chose to do rather than curl up and die.

I am not totally alone in what I am doing. I have had a lot of support from wonderful women. Tonight, my monthly group of Mormon, heretic, magnificent women is coming to my house. We are all active in the church and want to maintain that, and also want to keep our sanity and to transform the institution—to give our children the best of what we have, which is very good at its best, and to transform the worst of what we have, which can be very painful.

**Gay Lynn:** Sounds like you have had beautiful, loving, supportive friendships.

**Carol Lynn:** I have had very good friendships with like-minded women. Many of my Mormon women friends have dropped out of the church, and I can understand and honor that decision. It has not been my decision. I have plenty of Mormon women friends who have maintained in the church, who understand one another, and who give one another good support. That is part of the nurturing I continue to receive and it is a great support!

**David:** What does it feel like, being a woman doing this in the Mormon church?

**Carol Lynn:** It has been like walking a tightrope for years. Placing those steps very carefully, wanting very much not to fall off on one side or the other. And I have pulled it off quite remarkably.

A year ago, there were six Mormon feminist intellectuals who were excommunicated or disfellowshipped. That continues to happen. Last week a woman in Utah, who had been writing on the supposition that the Holy Ghost was really the missing Mother, was put on probation and may very well be excommunicated.

Now I have been fortunate. I have also been very careful. I have paid my dues in the church in terms of becoming a well-known and beloved figure in the church. My poems have been quoted for a long time by the highest sources. So that has placed me in an unusual position where I have had more voice, more freedom than most.

I have not attacked the church. I have always said good things about the church. I have done my work in a dignified fashion. I haven't gone out and chained myself to the Temple or anything outrageous. It has been a major challenge, and scary, but I have known from the start that this is what I am to do, this is what I came here to do.

Rather than be combative, I try to invite people on board with a new idea. I appreciate Joseph Campbell's statement when he said, "I would like to see people not leave their religion: I'd like to see them transform their religions."

**Gay Lynn:** And that's what you are doing; you're transforming your religion from within.

**Carol Lynn:** I have had considerable impact. Other women and men have had considerable impact. Some of it may not be seen for some time. There is a backlash in my church, as well as in society in general. And things right now are in some ways tighter than they have been.

> **I think what we are hearing is the death rattle of the patriarchy. They are trying to slam the barn door without realizing that the horse is long gone and there is no slamming that barn door! But there is such fear that, in desperation, that's all they know how to do!**

I think what we are hearing is the death rattle of the patriarchy. They are trying to slam the barn door without realizing that the horse is long gone and there is no slamming that barn door! But there is such fear that, in desperation, that's all they know how to do!

**Gay Lynn:** You are expecting a new grandchild; you already have another. What is your vision of the world for them?

**Carol Lynn:** I have to hope and believe for my grandchildren that the world is becoming a more habitable place in spite of everything I see—the gangs, the crime.

Everything we see could indicate that we are careening to an explosion that will destroy us all. If it's not nuclear, it will be social destruction. That may be, but I choose to believe that, on the other hand, there is enough enlightenment going on right now. I have to believe that good is more powerful than evil, or I would just curl up and die.

So I believe that the universe can create itself in a better, new way—that enough people are moving in a good direction and these two grandchildren of mine and whoever else comes along can find their particular gift to give and acknowledge the horror and pain that exist and say in spite of that, and because of that, here is my gift, which is something beautiful. And they give their beautiful gift to the world. Then I can have some peace of mind about leaving this world and watching them take over.

In the preface to *Mother Wove the Morning,* Carol Lynn shares:

*I anticipate in my hopes and my dreams, a time in years to come—who knows how many?—possibly fewer than we thought—in which women and men move solidly toward partnership together, acknowledging in their own partnerships the partnership of our Father and Mother God. In that day we will speak of and sing of and speak to a Creator in whose image we* all *are made equally.*

## Position

If "A" looks up to "B"
Then by nature of the physical universe
"B" must look down on "A"
Rather like two birds
Positioned
One on a tree
And one on the ground.

Or so thought Marjorie
Who had always wanted to marry
A man she could look up to
But wondered where that
Would place *her*
If she did.

Imagine her astonishment
When she met Michael and found
That together they stood
Physics on its head.

You could never
Draw this on paper
For it defies design

But year after year
They lived a strange
Arrangement
That by all known laws
Could not occur:

She looked up to him
And he looked up to her.

WOMEN I HAVE KNOWN AND BEEN
*CAROL LYNN PEARSON*

# 6

# Birthing God in Our Flesh: Incarnation

## Thoughts from David:

## Birthing God in Our Flesh: Incarnation

Babe Ruth, the home run king and hero of American boys, quit baseball at age 40 and died in what should have been his prime years. Why? Ty Cobb offers an explanation:

*He starts shoveling down victuals in the morning and never stops. I've seen him at midnight, propped up in bed, order six huge club sandwiches and put them away with a platter of pigs' knuckles and a pitcher of beer. And all the time, he'd be smoking big, black cigars.*

*Next day, he'd hit two or three homers and trot around the bases complaining all the way of gas pains and a bellyache. What might he have done if he would have taken even normal care of his body?*

*God's Key to Health and Happiness*
R. Josephson, 1962, Old Tappan, NJ: Fleming H. Revell

149

Our bodies are sacred. We incarnate the Divine—all of us. Most of Christianity has used the word "incarnation" to apply only to one holy man, but it rightfully is true of every woman, man and child. Holism and dualism are incompatible. Our body is of God, and therefore sacred, but humanity and the earth are sacred also.

> **Why have we thought so negatively and acted so destructively toward our bodies, humanity and the earth herself? Why are we so slow to hear and do something healthful in response to the cries of pain and suffering we inflict on ourselves, one another and our Mother?**

Why have we thought so negatively and acted so destructively toward our bodies, humanity and the earth herself? Why are we so slow to hear and do something healthful in response to the cries of pain and suffering we inflict on ourselves, one another and our Mother?

The word "symptom" is derived from the Greek word meaning "sign" or "signal." If the red oil-pressure light in a car goes on and off, we are alerted that the oil level is dangerously low and the engine needs the lubricant added immediately. If the light stays on, it is a warning of impending destruction. To ignore the signal is to invite the ruin of the engine.

Similarly, our bodies are exquisite energy in a manifest form that communicates constantly. We are alerted to the need to eat, to eliminate, to sleep and to drink. Babe Ruth had become so accustomed to self-abuse and pain, he just endured the suffering he caused himself as a part of his lot as a tough guy and real pro. Certainly no wimp or softy himself, the hard-driving, mean man of baseball, Ty Cobb, had the wisdom to know the destruction of the male body when he saw it.

We need to do some homework to see why and how we have come to such self-negating and destructive behavior toward ourselves, one another and the planet. That behavior has a long history, says Thomas Berry, stemming from our concept that the earth and all that's in it is something to be dominated rather than loved and cared for. "And God said to them, 'Be fruitful and multiply, and fill the earth and subdue it: and have dominion over the birds of the air and over every living thing that moves upon the earth'" (Genesis 1:28 RSV).

We have done our dominating and subduing. Now how about joining together and celebrating, preserving and reverencing, healing and loving?

Incarnation must be our guiding principle into wellness, wholeness, sacred oneness. We need to expand the celebration of incarnation beyond its application to only one man in history, "God being born in the flesh," and we must ascribe holiness to more than only certain avatars or saints.

Remember, the word "carnal" comes from the Latin *carnis,* which means "flesh." So "incarnation" means to be in the flesh. That Jesus, the Son of God, became flesh was the basis of a Christian theological doctrine. Jesus can be understood as God being birthed into an incarnation, and so can each of us as well.

The early church, and particularly the apostle Paul, viewed

> **Incarnation must be our guiding principle into wellness, wholeness, sacred oneness. We need to expand the celebration of incarnation beyond its application to only one man in history, "God being born in the flesh," and we must ascribe holiness to more than only certain avatars or saints.**

the flesh as the antithesis of spirituality. Carnal was often associated with all manner of human failing: "For while there is jealousy and strife among you, are you not of the flesh?" (I Corinthians 3:3 RSV).

For practical purposes, "flesh" and "sin" are synonymous even today in many churches. That which is of the flesh, the carnal, is lower, unspiritual, lustful, sexual, corrupting, ungodly, evil, sinful. Such dualism is not just found in conservative Christian churches; the God-Self and body also appear in a pervasive dichotomy of spirit and matter, taught in some of the metaphysical religions and courses that are often labeled New Thought or New Age today. Beyond the spiritual seekers of many different quarters, the general culture we live in fears, resists and wants to ban the body.

*The Phil Donahue Show* received letters protesting the airing of a videotape showing the birth of a child as obscene. The birth was seen as shameful, the result of a lewd and carnal act.

The divisions of dualism are artificial and unhealthy. The holistic person knows that we are a sacred spirit, soul, body. These are not three separate parts, but are like $H_2O$, which is manifested as steam, liquid and ice—all water, all the same elemental substance.

We have filled our thoughts, beliefs and patterns of living with disunity. We have divided our being into higher and lower parts. We have separated ourselves off from one another. After a young man was shot at the local high school, someone said to me, "I'm just glad it wasn't my boy." I thought, "He *was* our son—he belonged to all of us."

We saw a program on TV where two U.S. helicopters had been shot down by friendly fire in a stupid mix-up between the U.S. Army and Air Force. The parents and loved ones were furious. But if the helicopters had been occupied by the enemy—as defined by the government and military—no one would care, and the ones who shot them down would probably be regarded as heroes rather than culprits.

And our Earth? Is it Gaia? Is it a living, breathing, growing, nourishing, organic being? Thomas Berry, a profound philosopher of planetary spirituality who combines geology and theology and whimsically calls himself a "geologician," sees our relationship with God in three inseparable dimensions:

1. Divine—Human
2. Human—Human
3. Human—Earth

He points out that Western religion has dealt extensively with the first two dimensions and practically not at all with the third.

We live, move and have our being in a matrix of oneness. Our bodies are part of a larger body, the Earth, and all of this can be felt as the body of God.

Maybe we need to begin re-imaging and reverencing our bodies. That could help to heal us. That could affirm the incarnation.

One of our children ran naked outside on the front lawn when he was about two years old. This occurred in the mid-'60s, before *Hair* and Woodstock and all that supposed liberation. What a shock to see this bare-bottomed little boy cavorting on the well-kept lawn of a suburban subdivision. How embarrassing! Did any of the neighbors see him? How awful!

Why did it seem so terrible? How is it that, if he had happened to have been older, he would have been arrested? Why is not having clothes over certain parts of our body not just against cultural custom, but a criminal act? (And note that most of the time it is men who are arresting women for not being decent, just as it is men who are paying to see women dance without clothes in clubs because they are indecent.)

How deeply programmed we are with dualistic, anti-body attitudes. How repressed and contradictory! Is our Spirit good and our body bad? Are parts of our body good and parts bad? ("Don't touch that, Jimmy! Get your hand away from that. That's dirty!")

> **How deeply programmed we are with dualistic, anti-body attitudes. How repressed and contradictory! Is our Spirit good and our body bad?**

I went to an Esalen week with Sam Keen and John Heider in 1967. The experience changed my life. I experienced wonderful sitting and moving meditations where I became open to my body's flows. I came into the experience of my energy centers. I felt a whole new connection with my body as friend, companion. Before, ever since childhood, I had felt embarrassed and ashamed about my thin body; now I could look in the mirror and feel proud, okay, sacred. How healing that was and continues to be.

When I returned to the religious institution where I worked, some coworkers made snide remarks about my week at Esalen. "Did you go in the baths with no clothes on?" "Did you get a cheap thrill?" These remarks about the Japanese- or European-style baths at Big Sur's hot springs revealed the nervousness, repression and fears most people have about their own body, the temple of God.

Women in our society are starting to celebrate both the start of menstruation and that of menopause. Rites of passage that honor the woman's sacred flow are becoming healthy rituals for girls and elders, and all women and men.

The battle against the flesh has been waged mightily down through the history of the Christian church, where the words of the lower, lesser, corrupting part of ourselves are called "flesh," "sense," "carnal," "mortal," "worldly," and "human." Episcopal Bishop John Spong makes it clear that this rejection of our flesh as impure, unspiritual and sinful has deep roots in patriarchal traditions which oppressed the feminine and women. His insightful analysis of Mary the Mother of Jesus sheds light on how corrupted the belief is that Jesus could not have been conceived and born by natural means. He states in his book, *Born of a Woman—A Bishop Rethinks the Birth of Jesus:*

> *The more evil the flesh was thought to be, the more Mary's virtue needed to be protected. She became not just the virgin but the perpetual virgin and then the postpartum virgin. It became an issue of great import to prove that Mary retained her unbroken hymen through childbirth. The message that we are all born of God's Spirit was lost in a frenzy of patriarchal, anti-worldly literalism.*

The Bishop concludes:

> *I welcome the dawn of this deeper and higher human consciousness. The rewards that it will bring promise to be worth the journey we must make to a new Bethlehem, where we can once again worship and adore God who is met in the heart of our humanity incarnate. As male and female.*

Rejecting a literal interpretation of the Bible, Bishop Spong seeks to be a voice of wisdom and urges us to find the Spirit that is revealed in the Bible. He courageously explores subjects and refutes ideas that fundamentalists have adhered to and attempted to brainwash others into believing. Bishop Spong keenly re-examines the Bible and points out how outworn attitudes from that book have oppressed us, and also how we can see the Bible with a new, more honest, understanding of these Hebrew and Christian scriptures for our time.

Our interview with Bishop Spong is followed by a conversation with two Unity ministers, Pat and Jack Barker, wife and husband serving in Cincinnati, Ohio. The Barkers have used Bishop Spong's book, *Living in Sin—A Bishop Rethinks Human Sexuality,* as a text in classes they offer in their New Thought Unity Temple. They venture beyond traditional boundaries, daring to study the controversial issues John Spong raises about gays and lesbians in the churches, about nonmarried sexual relations, divorce, and how we can free ourselves from Bible literalism so we can be empowered to live in equal, nonexploitative, loving relationships.

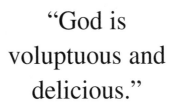

"God is
voluptuous and
delicious."

Meditations
with Meister Eckhart
—*Matthew Fox*

# Rethinking the Holy Family, with Bishop John Shelby Spong

John Shelby Spong, the Episcopal bishop of Newark, New Jersey, is an outspoken and controversial author of 14 books—including these bestsellers: *Rescuing the Bible from Fundamentalism, A Bishop Rethinks the Meaning of Scriptures, Living in Sin? A Bishop Rethinks Human Sexuality, Born of a Woman—A Bishop Rethinks the Birth of Jesus.* We focused on the latter two books, in which he applauds the fact that "the feminine aspect of God so long oppressed by the masculine patriarch is roaring back into our awareness, sweeping away our male prejudices and even our male definitions of the ideal woman."

John Spong has been a consecrated bishop since 1976. He has always had an active interest in sports and was at one time a radio announcer covering football, basketball and baseball.

Bishop Spong is an especially important voice today, standing against the bigoted, gay-bashing, "Let my conscience be your guide" crowd. Bishop Spong exposes to a wide audience ideas that many Bible scholars and clergy are already familiar with, but are reluctant to talk about publicly.

**Gay Lynn:** Our questions relate to the many helpful books you've written. We're particularly concerned about how

**Bishop John Shelby Spong**

the scriptural model for our families is based on a virgin mother and a celibate son. What has that supposition done to our understanding of spirituality and sexuality?

**Bishop Spong:** It has been quite negative, I believe.

**Gay Lynn:** How can we integrate our spirituality and sexuality, rather than deny or negate the latter?

**Bishop Spong:** We have to go back to the birth stories in the gospels and do a bit of historic analysis on them. The birth stories have profoundly impacted the role of women. When I wrote *Born of a Woman,* my whole purpose was to show that the placement of the virgin mother of the gospel into the ideal Christian family has had a rather horrendous effect on women throughout history.

But these birth stories are a late development in the Christian tradition. They are not original to that tradition. Paul was the first person to write in the New Testament, roughly between 49 and 62 C.E. There are two references to Jesus' origin in the whole Pauline corpus. One says he was born of a woman, like every other human being is born, without any explanation and certainly no birth story. In Romans he says that "according to the flesh" Jesus is descended from the seed of David. That indicates a pretty normal human process. Paul goes on to say that Jesus was declared "son of God" by "the spirit of holiness at the time of the resurrection," a rather interesting idea when you look at the later development of Christian theology.

In Mark's Gospel, which was the first gospel to be written, absolutely no story of Jesus' birth is included. Mark makes only two references to Jesus' family—one in chapter three and the other in chapter six. Both of them are negative.

Both portray his family as believing that Jesus was out of his mind, or as the text says, "beside himself," which is probably a Hebraism for "schizophrenic"! In one of those two texts, Mary is mentioned for the first and only time in Mark's Gospel when the crowd yells, "Is this not the son of Mary?" In fact that reference was itself pejorative, because when a grown Jewish male is called the son of a woman, it suggests that his paternity was questionable or unknown.

Now there is no Joseph and thus no father of Jesus at all in the first gospel. Joseph does not appear in a Christian text until the ninth decade. The first birth story is found in Matthew, written between 82 and 85 C.E. Joseph is the primary person in this story. (Mary becomes the primary person in the Gospel of Luke, written some five to 10 years later.) The Joseph story in Matthew is so obviously nonhistoric.

There are three things that Matthew says about Joseph. One is that Joseph had a father named Jacob. Secondly, everything that God says to Joseph comes through a dream; even the virgin birth text from Isaiah is communicated in a dream. Thirdly, Joseph's role in Matthew's drama was to save the child of promise from death by taking him down to Egypt.

When you go back to the Book of Genesis and read the story of Joseph who had a coat of many colors, you discover first that this Joseph had a father named Jacob; second, that he was overwhelmingly associated with dreams and was even called "the dreamer." By interpreting the Pharaoh's dreams, he achieved power in Egypt. Finally, Joseph's whole purpose in the drama of salvation was to save the people of the promise from death by taking them down to Egypt. Those things are not coincidental. There is a real question about whether the Joseph who appears in the New Testament was a legendary figure, created by the Christians to provide a father figure in a family where presumably one was not known.

Mary does appear in the Matthew story, and for the first and only time, the virgin text is introduced in the Bible. In a dream, God tells Joseph that Jesus' birth to a virgin had been anticipated in Isaiah 7:14. It is fascinating, however, that the word "virgin" is not in the original Hebrew text. The word *almah* is used in this text and *alman* never means "virgin" in the Hebrew language. It simply means "a woman."

This text was translated into Greek to accommodate the Jewish people in the Dispersion, around 250 B.C.E. Known as the Septuagint, that version uses the Greek word *parthenos,* which does have a virgin connotation. Unfortunately, Matthew only quoted the Greek translation of the Hebrew scriptures. He did not go back to the original Hebrew. So his whole virgin birth story was built upon a misunderstanding of a mistranslation of the Isaiah text.

Christianity had clearly moved a little bit out of the Jewish womb when Matthew wrote. It was a dozen to 15 years after the fall of Jerusalem. In the religious traditions and in the myths of the Mediterranean world, every great person was said to have been born of a virgin. So the virgin story entered Christianity from that perspective.

I suspect that behind the development of the virgin tradition was the fairly well-documented charge against Jesus by his Jewish critics that he was an illegitimate child, because the Jews believed that a religious agitator had to have been base born. They thought that is what made one a religious agitator.

**Gay Lynn:** These issues that you've touched on, which are so emotionally charged for us even today, all have to do with our sexuality—the necessity for having a virgin birth, the embarrassment of illegitimacy.

**Bishop Spong:** It also comes out of the negativity to women.

**Gay Lynn:** Exactly.

**Bishop Spong:** The virgin birth itself is sexist. It assumes a point of view in genetics where the woman is the receptacle of the whole life that is carried in the male seed. The woman does not contribute to that life.

Ancient people did not know about egg cells and zygotes and genetic codes. So when they wanted to talk about the Divine origin of a superhuman person, they never had to get rid of the woman because she did not contribute genetically to the life. They only had to get rid of the man and insert some power or Divine force in his place.

In 1827, the Western world finally discovered the egg cell. I mark that discovery as the beginning of the march into equality for women, because the masculine world had to acknowledge the fact that women were co-creators with males and not simply the vessels into which males planted new life. Prior to the discovery of the egg cell, the analogy was that of a farmer planting a seed in the soil of Mother Earth. Mother Earth did not add anything to the seed except the nurturing warmth of her body, and that is what they thought women did. So the very continuance of the virgin birth tradition perpetuates the idea that a woman is simply a receptacle for the gift of life that men plant in her. That is not the worst part of the virgin tradition for women, but that is something that needs to be confronted.

Once the virgin concept was brought into the Christian

church, the virginity movement began to grow. Mary got holier and holier, and loftier and loftier. By the time the church got through with developing the myth of Mary, she was immaculately conceived, a virgin mother, a postpartum virgin, and a perpetual virgin! It was even said that Jesus was born without disturbing Mary's hymen. In 1950, the church declared that Mary had been bodily assumed into heaven. That is, she did not really die.

> **This woman that the church has historically called "the ideal woman" is a person who has been dehumanized and desexed. Now I would like to ask: What is so evil about the humanity and the sexuality of a woman that before you can elevate her into godliness, you have to take her humanity and her sex away from her?**

This woman that the church has historically called "the ideal woman" is a person who has been dehumanized and desexed. Now I would like to ask: What is so evil about the humanity and the sexuality of a woman that before you can elevate her into godliness, you have to take her humanity and her sex away from her?

That is an example of the historic negativity toward women that the church has perpetuated. If you look back into the history of the church and find that the ideal woman is a virgin mother—which is rather difficult to be—then every other woman is reduced to being less than ideal. So the church has filled women with negativity and guilt and shame for just being women. Women have been taught to be ashamed and embarrassed about menstruation. It is called "an abomination" in the Bible. The myths that grew about menstruation were incredible. Women had done evil things, so their bodies had been mutilated. That was why they did not look like men. It was said that their bodies mourned the loss of their male organ by bleeding every 28 days. These stories are hilarious and could only have been written by men.

**Gay Lynn:** And the abuse and discrimination against women have been perpetuated by these negative attitudes, some of which are based in the Judeo-Christian scriptures.

**Bishop Spong:** Oh, absolutely. You see, if a virgin mother is the ideal woman, then no woman can achieve that ideal. This means that every other woman is inferior. The woman was taught to deal with her guilt by remaining a virgin and possibly becoming a nun, a holy woman, or by becoming a procreating mother. Those were the only two ways a woman could redeem her sinful, fallen, fleshly female body. Reproduction was defined as the only legitimate reason for sex. So if you ever put anything between sexuality and procreation, you committed a heinous sin. Thus the prohibition against birth control and abortion arises naturally out of the negative definitions of and attitudes toward women. Coming from this negative perspective, the church mandated in the 12th century that priests must be unmarried, celibate males.

**Gay Lynn:** And what does this do to our healthy sense of sexuality?

**Bishop Spong:** It tries to convince us that women are so corrupting that they cannot be related to holy men. If you want to be a holy man, you cannot be in a sexual relationship with a woman because she is evil and carnal. This means, of course, that if you feel any desire for a woman, it is the woman's fault. She has elicited this carnal desire from the holy man. That mentality simply permeates the Western Christian tradition. Many of these negative attitudes can be traced back to the birth narratives about Jesus and to the idealization of the Virgin Mary.

**Gay Lynn:** This negative attitude toward women has not only led to the persecution and discrimination of women, but has damaged the inner feminine in all of us—men and women.

**Bishop Spong:** I think the ultimate human power is to define what a human being is and gain acceptance of your definition. Armed with a book we Christians have called "the Word of God," which is overwhelmingly masculine and treats women as second-class citizens, we have imposed these prejudiced definitions upon the whole social order as God's will. Until very recently, we have forced women to accept these definitions and to live within them. Even in our time we find examples of hostility toward those women who step outside the traditional definition of what a woman is supposed to be. Look at the incredible hostility that has been heaped upon Hillary Clinton and the harassment directed at Geraldine Ferraro when she ran for vice president and later for the Senate— or any woman who had the audacity to claim some power in her own right.

The woman who dared to violate her culturally defined limits has had to pay a very big price. I have four daughters—one is vice president of a bank, one is an attorney teaching in law school, one has a Ph.D. and is a research physicist, and one has a degree in chemical engineering. They have all crashed into that glass ceiling on occasion and have had fascinating experiences.

**David:** Do you see resistance to the power of the feminine, particularly by the religious right? Can we have a fully sexual Mary, ordained women and homosexuals, sanctioned abortion, a woman president, ERA?

**Bishop Spong:** All of that is a consciousness war going on in this country as we speak. The religious right is at war with the emerging consciousness because it changes all the power equations that have served it well in the past. These are going to change dramatically. The old way of repressive and negative thinking about women and the feminine is doomed. Every year we have people die and new people enter the world.

My children laugh at old ways of hostile thinking toward women, often disguised as "family values." I am in favor of valuing our families, but we have to understand that families have changed dramatically. The world I live in is a place where, if you add up single parent families, single people, unmarried folks who are living together, and gay couples, these constitute the majority of families in America today. None of them is what we tend to call a traditional family.

The religious right keeps desperately trying to reimpose the old stereotype, but those stereotypes are dying. My mother, who is 89 years old, does not understand my daughters. Why do they want careers? Why aren't they happy just to be wives and mothers? That is what a woman is supposed to be, she thinks. She says, "I got married to have my husband's children," which I think is a very interesting and telling phrase. It reveals the image I referred to when I spoke about the seed being in the male, and the woman only being a receptacle.

**David:** We have a lot of challenges before us. We also see an interest in the power of women and the feminine spirit in all of us. We regard the feminine to be real, healing, helpful, comforting, creative, needed. How can we reawaken to an appreciation for the Divine Feminine in our lives and in our world?

**Bishop Spong:** You cannot suppress the feminine forever. We have tried to do this in Western society, but the feminine has interesting and perhaps even insidious ways of reasserting itself, like the yin and the yang. The yang cannot push the yin out of existence. The more it pushes, the more the yin rises on the other side. The feminine is in every human being, as is the masculine. If we can free the feminine in men, it would be a wonderful step forward. Men have a feminine side that has been suppressed because it has been unacceptable to express. Women certainly have a masculine side which also has been culturally unacceptable to express, so it has been repressed.

**David:** Is this where some of the negativity toward homosexual people comes from, the denial of the feminine and masculine in ourselves?

**Bishop Spong:** Yes, that is at least a part of it. This society rejects homosexual men far more than lesbian women. The ordinary definition of a homosexual is a man who acts like a woman in the sex act. So the assumption exists that any man who would be willing to act like a woman is just a dreadful, awful expression of humanity. Remember, we have this negative attitude toward women running all through our consciousness and culture.

**David:** So this negative attitude toward women and the feminine in general causes rejection of gay men.

**Bishop Spong:** Data, mostly from the brain sciences, indicate that sexual orientation is much like being left-handed. It has to do with the way the brain is organized in utero. Once this fact is recognized, the whole moral code about gay and lesbian persons will have to change, and it will. Sooner or later the church and the state will recognize and bless committed gay and lesbian unions. I expect that to come probably in my lifetime. The state will work that out first. Then all the legal, economical, political and social values of marriage will be applied to the partnerships of gay and lesbian people. In time the church will follow suit.

**David:** Some feminist theologians have suggested that maybe the reason there are more women than men in churches is that we're supposed to love the man, Jesus, to embrace the priest or pastor who is usually a man. We're supposed to love him and look up to him. Is there an unconscious reaction among men because this affection for another man raises homophobic fears?

**Bishop Spong:** I think that is true, and I think it also raises our unresolved Oedipus complex, particularly when the church has traditionally used the title "father" for its priests throughout Western history. Men are less comfortable relating to male figures called "father" than women are. My four daughters know how to get anything they want anytime they want it from me as their father. But they use the wiles taught them by the social order that oppressed people have always used. Dominant males would never be comfortable using those tactics.

One of the fascinating things I have noticed in the Episcopal church is that when we started ordaining women to the priesthood in 1977, we had difficulty deciding what to call the female priest.

**David:** You couldn't call her "father."

**Bishop Spong:** Right. But the people of the church could not bring themselves to call her "mother" either. Now fully 50 percent of our students studying for the priesthood are women. Twenty years from now the Episcopal priesthood will be a 50/50 profession, a fact that the people in the pew have not yet recognized.

**David:** So how do you resolve this?

**Bishop Spong:** The parental titles of "father" and "mother" are both disappearing, and overwhelmingly, the people in the congregation address members of the clergy by their first names. Those who want a formal title are most often called "pastor," which is thought to be sexually neutral.

**David:** In your book *Born of a Woman,* you give attention to the other Mary in the Christian scriptures—Mary Magdalene. You explore some scriptural clues which lead to the possibility that Jesus was married.

**Bishop Spong:** There is no question that Magdalene was a very significant figure in the Jesus movement. In every listing of women who followed and traveled with Jesus, Magdalene was always placed first. A woman got her status in the ancient world by being related to a very important man.

Jesus and his disciples had a group of women who were camp followers. You find them there with him as early as the Galilean phase of Jesus' ministry. People tend to become aware of the women first in the crucifixion and resurrection stories, when they took center stage. Yet they were always there.

A group of women following an itinerate male band of disciples in first century Galilee and Judea presents us with some very interesting images. These women in that culture had to have been their wives, prostitutes or, perhaps, mothers. As soon as you pose those images, even the most blatant right-wingers are happier with the idea that these women were wives rather than prostitutes.

In John's Gospel, Magdalene is portrayed as the chief mourner at the tomb. Why Magdalene? What was her role? She was mourning alone. She even referred to Jesus as "my Lord—They have taken away my Lord. . . ."

"My Lord" just happens to be the way a woman would address her husband in the polite society of Jewish culture. In John's Gospel, she demands to be shown where the body of Jesus was placed so that she, Mary Magdalene, can take that body away.

It would have been a scandalous act for a woman in first century Judea to claim the right to the body of a deceased Jewish male and not be the nearest of kin. So who was Magdalene? Also, in the New Testament, Jesus is repeatedly referred to as "rabbi." In Jewish society, a rabbi had to be married; it was a prerequisite. An unmarried man could not be a rabbi.

Those are only hints. I will have to wait until I get to the Kingdom of Heaven and interview a few people to get the proof. But you can make a very strong case for the existence of an intimate relationship between Jesus and Magdalene. I even argued in *Born of a Woman* that there is some reason to believe that the story of the wedding feast at Cana of Galilee was Jesus' own wedding. The real clue

in that story is that Mary, the mother of Jesus, was portrayed as the hostess who was responsible for the refresh-
ments. They went to her when the wine ran out. It makes
no sense to approach one of the guests when the wine runs
out. However, one could argue that Jesus had four brothers,
according to Mark's Gospel, and perhaps one of those
brothers was getting married. But Mary was clearly in the
mother-of-the-groom position.

Jesus has been portrayed through history as unmarried
because unmarried priests who did the portraying needed
Jesus as their role model. I think there is a real possibility
that Jesus was married and it got repressed in the church
tradition.

**David:** There are, of course, people who find that prospect
tremendously disturbing and repulsive. Why is this such a
bombshell for Christians?

**Bishop Spong:** If it is revolting to be married to a woman,
then one must ask what definition of a woman fills the
unconscious mind. What is so wrong with a woman that the
idea of a holy person being married is negative?

If I were going to tell you a dirty joke, you would expect
to hear a sex joke. It is interesting that our culture ascribes
"dirty" to the sexual act. But that negativity comes out of a
long history in which women have been defined as corrupters
and polluters of men. That is a very strange definition.

**Gay Lynn:** So how do we birth God in our flesh, rather
than divide our being into a spirit that is good and a body
that is lower? How do we help this incarnation to occur?

**Bishop Spong:** That is a good way to approach it. The reason I am a Christian and the reason the Christian story

appeals to me so powerfully is that at its heart and soul is the belief that every human being bears God's image. Therefore I must relate to every human being as if he or she were the bearer of the holy image. That means I cannot enslave, segregate, denigrate or treat as second-class citizens any human being —whatever that person is—a male, female, black, white, gay, straight.

The second thing the Christian faith tells me is that every human being is the object of the infinite

> **The reason I am a Christian and the reason the Christian story appeals to me so powerfully is that at its heart and soul is the belief that every human being bears God's image. Therefore I must relate to every human being as if he or she were the bearer of the holy image.**

love of God. The primary meaning of Jesus' life is that we cannot be or do anything that would place us outside the love of God. Betray God, you are loved. Deny God, you are loved. What more can we do? We try to kill the love of God and God responds by loving us! That is the Jesus story.

The third essential message of Christianity (and the one that makes most contact for me) is that the concept of Holy Spirit means that we are called, in the words of the Army commercial, to be all that we can be. That is what it means to be spiritual or to be whole. "Holy" means to be whole, to be free, to accept fully the fact that you are. It is to be like Popeye, who eats his spinach and says, "I yam who I yam"—that is the Christian affirmation. That means black people can say, "My God, black is beautiful!" That is whole and healthy. When gay people can say, "I am proud to be who I am, and I am not afraid to live out who I am with integrity," that is freedom. When a woman says, "I will not be defined by a man, especially by a tradition that sees me as subhuman and subservient," she is liberated. When a man says, "I will be all I can be as a man," then we have a whole, a new creation. That is what life in the Spirit is all about. That is why I stay in the Christian business. That is also why I take on the causes of civil rights, equality for women, and equality for gay and lesbian people. My present battle is to get rid of the anti-Semitism that lies so deeply in Christian scriptures. Anything that dehumanizes another person violates the gospel.

**Gay Lynn:** You know the story of the "Goose That Laid the Golden Eggs." How do you see us giving birth to our golden eggs?

**Bishop Spong:** My image of the church's role in life involves building an environment where people can be whatever God created them to be. People have thought that the way we become Christ-like is to imitate Jesus. Jesus was the Christ because he was everything he was meant to be. You and I come into Christ-likeness when we become everything we are meant to be. I was not created to be Jesus. I was created to be Jack Spong, and I want to be all that Jack Spong can be. I want to scale the heights and plumb life's depths. I want to love the realities of life and to exercise whatever power I have in such a way that everyone in the world can be free to be him- or herself. That is how I see us giving birth to our golden eggs.

It is okay to be
spiritual and sexual.

*Kansas City, Missouri*

# Reverends Jack and Pat Barker: The Power of Partnership

We caught up with Pat and Jack Barker, Unity ministers serving in Cincinnati, Ohio, at the Association of Unity Churches conference in Kansas City, Missouri. Pat was conducting a meeting as the president of the Board of the Association of Unity Churches. We began the interview with Jack, and Pat joined us after her meeting was adjourned.

As friends and colleagues, Pat and Jack have been a joyful part of our lives and spiritual journeys. We chose to interview them because we saw in them a beautiful example of how they honored the Divine Feminine and Masculine within themselves and in each other. In a marriage that spans over 30 years, and a co-ministry that has flourished more than 27 years, they have demonstrated the partnership model that is equally honoring, loving, and enduring.

**Gay Lynn:** Is it possible that Jesus was married?

**Jack:** If Jesus were not married, he would have been breaking Hebrew policy as a rabbi. Donovan Joyce systematically showed in his book, *The Jesus Scroll,* who Jesus' wife was, who his son was—at least one of them that

**Pat and Jack Barker**

we know of—and the whole process of how that can be true. And being somewhat of a Bible scholar (I don't look at myself as any expert), I wondered, "Did I miss that?" But the book describes these things in terms of Hebrew tradition, which I didn't know about. But the stories are there.

**David:** So the idea of Jesus having a wife, a partner—why is this relevant for our lives today?

**Jack:** Well, it's important to me because it suggests or substantiates that Judeo-Christian tradition has written the feminine out of the literature. They have pushed the women out of the priesthood. They have denigrated them. And they have made them of lesser importance. And, my gosh! That has had an impact in our society and the role of women from that time forward. Of course, you know we are fighting this battle on a daily basis. We are fighting the battle to somehow bring the Divine Feminine, the mystery, the mysticism back into our religion.

> It's important to me because it suggests or substantiates that Judeo-Christian tradition has written the feminine out of the literature. They have pushed the women out of the priesthood. They have denigrated them. And they have made them of lesser importance. And, my gosh! That has had an impact in our society and the role of women from that time forward. Of course, you know we are fighting this battle on a daily basis. We are fighting the battle to somehow bring the Divine Feminine, the mystery, the mysticism back into our religion.

One of the major points of focus for Unity and for religion in general is to look at ourselves and ask, "What have we done to ourselves?" How have we disenfranchised 50 percent of our population, the women? Because we have taken this tack that they are not important. I believe a lot of ills of humankind are based on the fact that we have set women and the feminine aside. We have allowed brutality toward women, we have put them in subservient roles, and this has really made things a mess! I think our society would be much more loving, gentle and nurturing if we had not lost the Divine Feminine, and I think it is high time we put it back in.

**David:** We have done research that suggests women were disciples.

**Jack:** There were women disciples, but you wouldn't know that unless you read the Nag Hammadi Library or the Dead Sea Scrolls. Some discount them. They say, "Oh, that's those Gnostics. They didn't know what they were doing." But they really knew what was going on in their time. And we can say because of them, "Women disciples—that's not so far-fetched an idea after all."

**Gay Lynn:** The Gospel of Philip said the "companion of the Savior is Mary Magdalene. But Christ loved her more than the other disciples, and used to kiss her often on her mouth. The rest of the disciples were offended . . . . They said to him, 'Why do you love her more than all of us?' The Savior answered and said to them, 'Why do I not love you as I love her?'" This is a refreshing portrayal of a human Jesus who shared his love with Mary Magdalene.

**David:** What are some practical ways you have translated this into your ministry?

**Jack:** We have de-genderized our language. God is not so much Father/Mother. Instead of using male and female terms, which are uncomfortable for some, we take God as principal, as essence, that which underlies everything. To that there is no gender applied. In that awareness we de-genderized our hymns, and before we read the Scriptures, we rewrite them. We take out the male specific language or we don't use it. If it doesn't lend itself to be literally changed, we use something else. In everything we do, we have changed the language, not just because my partner is a female. We have attempted to make that an absolute part of our ministry. It is to the point in the church that, when a hymn squeaks through that has not been changed, we hear about it from the women in the congregation. I think we need to be 10 steps ahead of the leading edge in language usage.

> **De-genderized language is inclusive language in the way that we use it. Instead of saying "he" or "she," we use "we" or "ours." "Our Father" becomes "Our God" in the Lord's Prayer. We use a language that includes everybody and leaves no one out.**

De-genderized language is inclusive language in the way that we use it. Instead of saying "he" or "she," we use "we" or "ours." "Our Father" becomes "Our God" in the Lord's Prayer. We use a language that includes everybody and leaves no one out.

**David:** In your personal life, in your family and marriage, does including the feminine allow for greater expression?

**Jack:** Absolutely. As a male—and I can only speak from that perspective—it has opened up in my nature more than I could have thought possible. And it has caused me to re-examine what I am as a man. There is a side of me as a Judeo-Christian male that didn't even consider a Divine Feminine as an aspect within me. All of a sudden I became aware of a whole side of my nature that I had never looked at. I started to do some self-examination. I asked myself, "Am I really able to stay in touch with this part of myself?" Oftentimes the answer is "No," because the other is so deeply ingrained that I have trouble with it. But at least I am aware of the Divine Feminine part of myself, and I recognize when I am out of tune with that part of my nature. That is a pretty good step down the road. Even when I make a mistake—"Oops, you did it again!"—I recognize it and try harder to consciously change the old pattern. This has made me aware of a side of my nature I have never touched, and I am trying to touch that daily.

*[Pat has now joined us in the interview.]*

**Gay Lynn:** Can you respond to this, Pat? How has your relationship with Jack been affected by this awareness?

**Pat:** I think as a male is willing to look at the Divine Feminine within himself, it makes it safe for and empowers his partner to look at the Divine Masculine in her own self, to become a more balanced person. We both are better off because of our willingness to look at the different aspects of the divine in each other.

As for the ministry, it helps in a subtle way for the congregation that we serve. There is the Divine Feminine as well as the Divine Masculine, and God is genderless. And we need to address all the aspects of our whole nature, and not just look at this slotted way of approaching God as masculine.

**David:** Can you give us any examples of how you model and project that message to your congregation in your ministry together?

**Jack:** Our ministry has been a balance of the male and female energies. I have been greatly influenced by Pat and she has helped me develop a new pattern of tempering what I do.

At one time in my life—10 or 20 years ago—I would have dealt with a situation in my life in a totally different way. Pat has helped me not only to be aware of the Divine Feminine, but also to be balanced by her. It has changed me a lot! Pat has helped to model that for me, and I hope together we have modeled that for our congregation.

**Pat:** I think we have to a large extent, because we have a great number of professional people in our congregation. A couple of attorneys who come regularly have shared with me that they come to the church because it is a good balance for their lives. All week long they operate out of the harsh, dictatorial, patriarchal side of themselves, and coming to church helps them to balance with the side of themselves that is more in balance with their loving, compassionate and accepting natures.

I think because we are willing, month after month and year after year, to share and model as equally as we can that there are other ways of looking at God and relationship and life, it helps people recognize their own wholeness.

I think I am more whole because of the way we share in our ministry and our life, and our congregation experiences that as well.

**David:** There are very few churches where people can walk in and see a man and woman sharing the ministry as equal partners—spiritual, human and professional equals. We have a unique distinction and it makes a great impact on people.

**Jack:** Oh, yes. As a matter of fact, some people have said to us that they found our ministry so meaningful in their lives because they can tell their friends, "Look—we have both the male and female represented in our church, and they are both honored."

**Pat:** And both aspects of our being are honored as well, and I think that is important. I think we are in a wonderful time. I look at our daughter, who is now 30, and she is a young professional vice-president of a bank and trust. That is a very responsible position for someone her age—but I feel that she has a more balanced beingness. She has watched through the years that it is okay to be strong, but also tempered, to be compassionate and also intelligent, to be loving and also firm—not aggressive, but firm. I think she has made a difference in her profession because they have watched these qualities in her emerge.

I hope the younger men in our congregation will honor their feminine side and the younger women will honor their masculine side in a more balanced way.

**Gay Lynn:** We believe that it is from this balanced nature inside of us that we give birth. Can you share some examples of this in your lives?

**Pat:** In the Sunday services we create, there is a dance of energy that we share between the two of us. It serves as yeast, to give rise to that spirit we share together.

**Jack:** All of our services are that way. They come out of our collective consciousness rather than out of either one of us. We develop our services that way.

**Gay Lynn:** What do you see as the next leap in consciousness for our human evolution?

**Pat:** We have spent the last 300 to 400 years perfecting our sciences, aiming to live more comfortably, to manufacture great things. And we are still not happy. We are not kind to each other, and we are not compassionate to one another. For me, it is because we have left out the feminine, that compassionate element. We wrote it out of history. Now it is time to write it back into history so that we have a balance.

**Gay Lynn:** If we find ourselves acting really aggressive and assertive, how can we balance that in our lives?

**Pat:** Whether they be male or female, when people are aggressive, it is because they are unsure of who they are. They feel they must perform, they must show off, they must win at all costs. When they come to realize it's not outer accomplishments or winning the race, that there is something deep within them that is priceless, worthy, holy, then they don't have to prove anything to you or to anyone. They don't have to compete, to run the race and win top honors. It encourages them to look at their inner nature and worth and value as a person—not hiding from the loving, compassionate part of themselves.

> **Whether they be male or female, when people are aggressive, it is because they are unsure of who they are. They feel they must perform, they must show off, they must win at all costs.**

**David:** What is your response to some of the research that suggests that Jesus was married?

**Pat:** I find it positive to know that the "way-shower" lived the kind of life we are living. The fact that he dealt with some of the same kinds of challenges and was aware of what it was like to be in a human relationship, as well as in a holy, sacred relationship with God, is really comforting. Because I, too, can make my life work more successful.

**Jack:** The priest that has said to the woman that she must have another child, or she cannot practice birth control, or she can't get out of an abusive marriage because of the church doctrines—all this is coming from a person who has never been any part of that way of life. I have a tremendous conflict with that. Who are they to tell me what this is about, having never experienced it themselves?

To find out that the one who said, "Love one another" was practicing that as each of us have to in the nitty-gritty of daily contact with another person—that makes it much more meaningful.

**Gay Lynn:** If Jesus were married, he probably would have been engaged sexually. We have a lot of problems because of the way our sexuality has been split off and not fully embraced.

**Pat:** John Shelby Spong has done a wonderful job looking at that in his book, *Living in Sin? A Bishop Rethinks Human Sexuality.* Jack and I taught a class on it in our church. It involves looking at our own human sexuality and the myths that we have been living with because of our Judeo-Christian background and the Hebrew scriptures. He explodes those myths and allows us to view our sexuality from a very different perspective. And he looks at how women have been abused in history and allowed to be abused because of our Judeo-Christian background and the Hebrew scriptures.

**David:** How does it hurt us when we have a celibate son and a virgin mother as our role models?

**Jack:** It really messes up our lives! It really does.

**Pat:** It is so unreal!

**Jack:** If there is that specialness about them, then, to me, it makes them irrelevant. To say these two people were special in this way is to set up conflicts that cannot be resolved because we cannot relate to them.

**Gay Lynn:** So having a Jesus with a sexuality makes him more relevant to our lives?

**Jack & Pat:** Oh, yes!

**Pat:** Because if he dealt with issues in his own life and came to a center within himself that he was consequently transformed by, then I, too, have hope. We all have hope of touching that same center, expanding into it, and finding our own lives transformed in the same way.

**Gay Lynn:** So if our sexuality and spirituality are not in separate boxes, how do we live this in our daily lives?

**Jack:** I think we need to be aware that it is not something apart from our spiritual life. If people were to honor their sexuality as part of their spirituality, it would immediately transform the abuse that is brought about by the misconceptions. If you make every sexual experience a spiritual experience of wholeness, it would bring about a wholeness in the people involved in it. We would put our sexuality and our spirituality on an entirely different level.

We wouldn't be using or abusing another person. It would transform all of that, and it would be done as a ritual.

**Pat:** Or a gift of love, or a recognition of holiness.

**David:** As ministers, we are often thought of as not having a sexual life. We are not supposed to talk about sexuality in church, about things from our "lower nature."

**Jack:** We would immediately throw out that statement "lower nature," that our sexuality has anything to do with our lower nature. I am a spiritual being having a human experience, and all of my human experience is made spiritual by who I am as a spiritual being. We will heal that

> I think we need to be aware that it is not something apart from our spiritual life. If people were to honor their sexuality as part of their spirituality, it would immediately transform the abuse that is brought about by the misconceptions. If you make every sexual experience a spiritual experience of wholeness, it would bring about a wholeness in the people involved in it. We would put our sexuality and our spirituality on an entirely different level.

consciousness and throw those kinds of teachings out once and forever. We don't have to talk about our sex life on Sunday, but we can certainly address in our churches the honoring of the fact, "I am a spiritual being having a human experience, and that includes my sexuality."

**Pat:** And we cannot extricate our sexuality from our human expression. It is a gift, and to recognize it fully is to honor it. As Jack said, it becomes a holy experience, not something experimental or done from lust.

**Gay Lynn:** We see a separation being made between spirit and matter. Spirit is good and matter is thought of as being evil, carnal, of the flesh.

**Pat:** How can that be? It is all God!

**Jack:** In quantum physics today we have gone beyond the atom as the smallest particle, and we are getting down to deeper and deeper levels. In our atomic structure we are mostly space and all that space is filled with God. And all of the matter we are composed of has within it life substance and intelligence. We are spiritualizing everything because we are spiritual beings. Spirit has already done that for us. What we need to do is recognize that it is there. We become aware that we are that spirit that animates us!

# A Woman Waits for Me

A woman waits for me, she contains all, nothing is lacking,
Yet all were lacking if sex were lacking, or if the moisture of
the right man were lacking.
Sex contains all, bodies, souls,
Meanings, proofs, purities, delicacies, results, promulgations,
Songs, commands, health, pride, the maternal mystery, the
seminal milk,
All hopes, benefactions, bestowals, all the passions, loves,
beauties, delights of the earth,
All the governments, judges, gods, follow'd persons of the
earth,
These are contain'd in sex as parts of itself and justifications
of itself,
Without shame the man I like knows and avows the
deliciousness of his sex,
Without shame the woman I like knows and avows hers.

LEAVES OF GRASS
BY WALT WHITMAN

# 7

# You Must Be Born Again and Again and Again

## You Must Be Born
## Again and Again and Again

I live on Earth at present,
And I don't know what I am.
I know that I am not a category.
I am not a thing—a noun.
I seem to be a verb,
an evolutionary process—
an integral function of the universe.

(Old World Order:)
Newton: a body persists in a state of
rest or constant motion except as it is
affected by other bodies. The normal
condition of all things is inertia.
(New World Order:)
Einstein: All bodies are constantly
being affected by other bodies. Their normal
condition is continuous motion and change.

I SEEM TO BE A VERB
BY BUCKMINSTER FULLER

You have all heard the saying, "You must be born again." You see it on billboards, bumper stickers and religious tracts all the time. Some people claim to be born again and ask if you have been born again. Does this only refer to a particular experience, or does it have a larger meaning as an ongoing renewal of life? You all have been born from your mother's womb, but what is this process of being born again?

A wonderful discussion takes place between Jesus and the searching Pharisee, Nicodemus (John 3:1-21). Nicodemus is a religious leader of high position and authority, member of the ruling Sanhedrin, the highest court and council of the ancient Jewish nation. He comes to see Jesus at night, under cover of darkness, presumably to escape the notice of gossips, who might otherwise see him seeking out the controversial teacher and healer from Galilee.

Nicodemus recognizes that this man, Jesus, must have found something because of the results that he gets when he works with people. Jesus sees that Nicodemus is a seeker, and they engage in a fascinating conversation about who we are and how we develop and grow. Jesus tells the Pharisee that we have to be born over again (and again and again), out of our old ways of thinking, feeling, acting and reacting. Nicodemus may have been steeped in traditions, customs, hierarchies, rigid ways of thinking and doing things, and Jesus could see this.

Nicodemus has trouble understanding how we can be born again and asks how a grown person can go back into the mother's womb to be born a second time. He perceives him-self as a physical body who came from his mother. Jesus sees himself and Nicodemus as whole beings—of Spirit, soul, body—who birth themselves continually.

Jesus implies that our parents made it possible for us to acquire a physical form, a body. We have all been born of a woman, including himself. (At least Jesus never said that he had been born in any way other than the natural way everyone gets born in this world.)

We have this body—a marvelous flesh-and-blood incarnation of energetic life. Our parents facilitated our forming our bodies and our births into these human forms on this planet.

They may have told us, "I gave you life." That is, "Our bodies came together and created you, gave you life, 'made' you. We made a baby, and that is 'you.'" If they had some heavy control needs, they may even have thrown in occasional guilt and obligation with something like, "We gave you your life and you owe us."

To quote Kahlil Gibran in *The Prophet:*

> *Your children are not your children.*
> *They are the sons and daughters of*
> *Life's longing for itself. They come*
> *through you but not from you,*
> *and though they are with you, yet*
> *they belong not to you.*

You may have the honor and joy to help in the birthing and caring for children. Through love and wisdom you fulfill your parenting relationship as guide, model, protector, teacher, helper, counselor, student and friend. You realize there is a lot more to parenting than having a baby.

Nicodemus perceives himself as a physical being who came from his mother. Jesus sees him as a whole person who was born of God *through* his mother and father, and who is now birthing himself continually. You must be born again, and again, and again. Jesus tries to make Nicodemus realize the eternal birthing that can take place as a self-renewing process. You give your body life according to your consciousness of the Life of Spirit and your ability to let it flow through you like the wind through the trees. "Do not be astonished," says Jesus to Nicodemus and us, "that I said to you, you must be born from above (or anew). The wind (or 'Spirit') blows where it chooses, and you hear the sound of it, but you do not know where it comes from or where it goes. So it is with everyone who is born of the Spirit" (John 3:7-10 NRSV). Like the ancient Chinese philosopher, Lao-Tzu, Jesus has insight into the creative flow of life.

Empty
yourself
of everything
Let the mind rest in peace.
The ten thousand things rise and fall
while the Self watches their return.
They grow and flourish
and then return to the source.
Returning to the source is stillness,
which is the way of nature.
And though the body dies,
the Tao
will never
pass
away.

TAO TE CHING
*LAO-TZU*

Be in this renewing, healing flow, Jesus counsels. You *are* the Life of Spirit seeking to express wholeness through you, ever more fully *as* you. The way of living and loving well involves many rebirths.

You are born again and again and again. Your life is an ongoing, self-renewing journey through many stages, cycles, passages, loves, works, deaths, good-byes, realizations, regenerations, rebirths.

> **Your life is an ongoing, self-renewing journey through many stages, cycles, passages, loves, works, deaths, good-byes, realizations, regenerations, rebirths.**

The basic healing, transforming insight here is that *I* give my body life; it does not give *me* life. I *am* the life my body expresses. I am still birthing my body and my living daily.

Since being born again has been considered by some as necessary for salvation, you need also to take a look at what that really means. Salvation comes from the Greek word *salvos,* which means "to heal or make whole." We get the word "salve," a healing ointment, here also. There is no indication of being saved from punishment in an afterlife or even that one has to accept Jesus Christ as Savior. The word "savior" may take on a different meaning for you if you know it means "healing person," or "one who helps bring wholeness." Wholeness and holiness are the same.

Another well-known statement follows the Jesus and Nicodemus encounter. This passage is considered by many scholars to have been added and not to be from Jesus directly. However, since it has been so widely quoted, usually to try to force people to be saved in a certain way, we need to consider it not as a doctrinal statement used to intimidate, but as another wise saying about our eternal birthing process. Eric Butterworth comments with keen insight on this familiar text:

> *The verse of the Scripture most commonly uttered by "salvationist" Christian preachers has been John 3:16: "For God so loved the world, that he gave his only begotten Son, that whosoever believeth in him should not perish, but have everlasting life." (KJV) This has been cited as positive proof of the divinity of Jesus, and of his special dispensation as the Son of God. However, note how this takes on new meaning when we see it through the perception of Meister Eckhart, one of the great Christian mystics of the Middle Ages. He says that God never begot one Son, but the eternal is forever begetting the only begotten.*
>
> *The "only begotten" is the spiritual human, the Christ nature, the principle of the divinity of humankind. The "only begotten son" is that which is begotten* only *of God. There is that in all of us that is begotten of many sources. One person may be begotten of an alcoholic father and thus appear to repeat his traits of weakness. Others may be begotten of ancestors who have history of a certain disease, so they accept this as their lot in life. And many of us are subliminally begotten of the exploitation by advertising in newspapers, magazines, radio and television—so that we develop the motivations that business is cultivating for its own profit.*
>
> *But John 3:16 is saying, "God's love is so great, God's wisdom so infinite, that God has given to humankind that which is so pure and perfect, that which is begotten* only *of God. No matter what we may experience, you are a child of God, and you always have*

*within you the infinite potential of the Christ.*

*"Those who believe this about themselves—really believe that they are 'the inlet and may become the outlet of all there is in God'—will not die but have everlasting life." This is not a proof of Jesus' divinity. It is rather a restatement of his discovery of the divinity of humankind, which he proved. He discovered that in himself which was begotten only of God, and he believed it so completely that even death and the tomb could not hold him.*

*Discover the Power Within You*
Eric Butterworth, 1968, Harper Collins

Meister Eckhart once said:

What good is it to me
if this eternal birth of the divine Son
takes place unceasingly
but does not take place
within myself?

And,
what good is it to me
if Mary is full of grace
and if I am not also full of grace?
What good is it to me
for the Creator to give birth to his/her Son
if I do not also give birth to him

in my time
and my culture?
  This, then,
is the fullness of time;
When the Son of God
is begotten
in us.

MEDITATIONS WITH MEISTER ECKHART
*MATTHEW FOX, BEAR & CO.*

Work with these affirmations and be born again and again:

I am begotten of God.

I value and celebrate myself as a growing child of God.

I am born again and again and again.

I am not stuck or static or fixed but am free to grow in maximum ways.

I am genesis and I am genius.

The Creator (Creative Process) is always, eternally, at birth in me.

To be in that
place of delivery is
to be in a space of
non-control.

*Berkeley, California*

# Patricia Sun:
# Naturally Birthing Ourselves

We sat in the home of Patricia Sun high in the Berkeley, California hills. The transpersonal psychologist and lecturer on natural childbirth at the University of California-Berkeley shared her thoughts on the physical and metaphysical birth process.

**Patricia:** The more wisdom that we have about the birthing process, the more we are able to center ourselves in ourselves. We are not afraid, and we move confidently through the stages and perceive clearly the rise of the new life within us. The psychology and physiology of an actual birth is a mirror of the same creative process we need to go through. In both places we make some of the same mistakes because of our style of thinking.

There is a new way of holding reality, information, of using both hemispheres of the brain so that they work together more respectfully of each other. This is the next level of thinking when your intuitive mind and linear logical mind don't fight each other. When they are both mature in us there is an honoring and consciousness about the different styles, which creates a quantum leap in awareness. The actual stages

**Patricia Sun**

of giving birth are a metaphor for becoming conscious, for giving birth to yourself, from one state to another.

> **The actual stages of giving birth are a metaphor for becoming conscious, for giving birth to yourself.**

**Gay Lynn:** How can we begin this maturation process and honor both our intuitive and logical minds, or what we call the Divine Feminine and the Divine Masculine?

**Patricia:** Moving to the next level requires a respect for the gestation time and connection, when it looks like nothing is happening. Usually we are pulling up the seed and saying, "Are the roots growing yet?" And then we are destroying it and breaking the connection. The main enemy of birth is premature labor. This is labor which begins before the gestation is complete.

> **Moving to the next level requires a respect for the gestation time, when it looks like nothing is happening. Usually we are pulling up the seed and saying, "Are the roots growing yet?" And then we are destroying it. The main enemy of birth is premature labor.**

**Gay Lynn:** It's easy to relate this to our lives. We have a dream, an idea, a way we would like to connect with the world and those around us, and we need to protect that for a period of gestation so that it can become vital and strong and have a life of its own. Often we prematurely share a plan, a desire, a need to let go of old fears and habit patterns, and it is met with: "You have got to be kidding!" "You can't do that." "Who do you think you are?" "What would you want to do that for?" These and other such statements harm the new life which intuitively knows when it needs to be delivered. You're saying we need to let this developing idea gain its fullness and come forth naturally when it's ready.

**Patricia:** Yes, that involves trusting God, nature, the universe, ourselves, and we have very little trust in all of that. We are in a control mode or a despair mode. The linear mind fears the intuitive mind. It feels anxious, wants to know the plan, the journey, what's next. Impatience always slows things down. The fastest way is being patient, being respectful of nature, of the process, of individuals, of yourself and your own process. And in that respect a genuine connection can be made, and you feel an inner way of knowing what can be done. There is a gentle prodding so that we don't have to make it into a drama or a disaster.

> Yes, that involves trusting God, nature, the universe, ourselves, and we have very little trust in all of that. We are in a control mode or a despair mode. The linear mind fears the intuitive mind. It feels anxious, wants to know the plan, the journey, what's next. Impatience always slows things down.

Respectful interactions are essential. If we could look on all interactions as little births, and respectfully interact and take the time to feel the other person and have them feel us, and really know what's going on, all things are solvable.

The hallmark of the evolutionary leap is being connected and tuned in, and it's a reciprocal, interactive experience. The more you choose it the more it offers the opportunity for the other person to respond to you in kind.

Likewise, the converse is true about what I call matching energy. If you have a sarcastic tone, or even if you don't but you are thinking, "This person is a jerk"—even if you say the right words—the person will resent what you said, not fully hear you, or become defensive. Then you are into the victim/victimizer dance and the respect for the individual is gone, and they for you.

What happens is that we are constantly giving birth to the adult part of ourselves that is taking care of the wounded and child parts of ourselves. Every person on this planet has parts that aren't grown-up. It is important now that we are all giving birth to our species.

We cannot build enough prisons to control all dysfunctional behavior. We heal dysfunctional behavior by changing it in ourselves, by making it more socially normal to be healthy instead of socially normal to be doing obviously dysfunctional things, like drinking and abusing children. We need to self-correct.

**David:** Sometimes when birth is taking place in someone's life, it's difficult. A person may go to the doctor with symptoms of that difficulty, such as, "I am having trouble sleeping," "I'm very tense and anxious," or "I'm depressed and disoriented." These symptoms are related to the major life changes or new birth that is taking place. The medical person might give the person pharmaceuticals that make that person feel different, just as the obstetrician may anesthetize the mother completely so she doesn't have to participate in the birth of her child. Most births, whether physical or spiritual, work better when the person is conscious and in touch with what's going on. To be present and participating is most rewarding for the person in labor and for that which is being brought forth. Not just going through it, but growing and glowing through it, as difficult as it may be.

**Patricia:** Often labor is feared. The pain is activated by the fear. If we look at the pain with understanding, there is less stress, and when we work with the process the delivery is natural. In physical delivery, the uterine muscle, the main muscle that helps in labor and delivery, is involuntary. Normally we think of not having any influence over involuntary muscles, but we can assert considerable influence over these muscles through relaxation. Fearfulness tightens this set of muscles.

We also have involuntary responses to life that we can handle much more effectively by breathing and relaxing. We also need to feel safe in an environment with people who help us feel secure, at peace, and who care about us. The inner part of us knows that there is only one contraction at a time.

As we stay in the current of the contraction, breathe, relax, we bring forth what is being birthed naturally. I believe that at birth and death we are at the portals of coming in and going out, and at these transformational points of our lives we are psychically most open.

During the delivery you have to remind yourself not to push too hard. When you push too hard you get into that disconnected off-balance place, which creates pain, injury

> **During the delivery you have to remind yourself not to push too hard. When you push too hard you get into that disconnected off-balance place, which creates pain, injury and slows down the process.**

and slows down the process. The actual stages of giving birth are a metaphor for becoming conscious, of giving birth to ourselves. If you begin to feel the energy and anxiety building, you are uncomfortable, fearful, and you feel in pain. To be in that place of delivery is to be in a space of non-control. Let the moment rise and fall. Stay present with the moment and be connected to it consciously, doing the best you can. This is ultimately the way of enlightenment.

**Gay Lynn:** We are spiritual obstetricians and midwives of the soul, as Socrates said. We get into trouble when we want to control what comes out and how it is going to come, and resist life opening us to a larger dimension. Perhaps we force something or someone else that is not meant to be—like a relationship that we push into being a certain way, causing ourselves and others much pain. What if he leaves me? What if she loves someone else? What if I end up alone? What if he doesn't do what I want him to do? What if she betrays my trust again? What if I screw up really badly? Fear restricts us and the window of enlightened birth is slammed shut.

**Patricia:** We need to approach birth in a nonviolent and uncontrolling way, and breaking connection from awareness of the natural order. All violence and control are related to being unconscious and afraid. We are not aware of who we are or our power and ability. We have believed a terrible, unkind lie about ourselves, and that is we see ourselves as powerless. We are most afraid of that place of surrender. We need to break through to that natural order, then we can let go and breathe through the peak of life's contractions with balance. It is much easier to go through those scary places when we have an open heart to the natural order (or God). We can do our planning, we can be knowledgeable and even logical, but ultimately we let go to cooperate with life, and what may have been a crisis is actually a birthing of divine insight and growth.

**David:** When people started crying in the days of the encounter and sensitivity groups, it was common for someone to put their arms around them and try to comfort away the tears. However, when I took Journal Workshops with Dr. Ira Progoff, he would usually hold up his hand to keep someone seated so they would not go over to soothe away someone else's pain or tears. That let the person honor his or her own struggle, grief, birthing process—by being present with the sadness in the painful contraction of life's labor. Even running over to someone with a handful of Kleenex is an unconscious way of saying, "Wipe that away," or "Clean up your face; you don't want to appear messy."

**Patricia:** And yet we all know that birth is messy. It's noisy. It isn't without blood and sweat, but it is magical to experience, and we often can see the magic of the transformation as we allow for the full delivery of the experience. Some people are afraid to let go—they fear they will begin to cry and not be able to stop. We often hold ourselves back, filter it, clamp down, and there is this huge energy that needs to be released.

Sometimes we are afraid we will be overwhelmed, and rarely, if ever, is this the case. The opposite occurs when we fuse our feelings with compassion and awareness. When we connect to ourselves and one another in a safe, secure, supportive way, we can move through the pains of life's contractions, breathe, relax, release and deliver ourselves to a new emotional life of freedom.

I birth
inner peace
by letting go
of fear.

*Tiburon, California*

# Jerry Jampolsky and the Abundance of Creativity

To behold Jerry Jampolsky, M.D. today and to know of the countless lives he has touched with love and peace make it hard to believe that this psychiatrist's life years ago was falling apart from alcohol, fear and atheism. While on this path of self-destruction, he was introduced to a set of books, *A Course in Miracles.* After experiencing a profound spiritual awakening, Jerry, with the help of many children and parents, formed Attitudinal Healing networks composed of young people with life-threatening illnesses.

Jerry is founder of the Center for Attitudinal Healing in Tiburon, California. Today more than 100 such centers exist in cities and towns around the world. On demand worldwide for speaking engagements before medical and general audiences, Jerry has also appeared numerous times on the national talk-show circuit. He is author of several books, including *Love Is Letting Go of Fear, Teach Only Love, Goodbye to Guilt, There Is a Rainbow Behind Every Dark Cloud,* and *Me First and the Gimme Gimmes* (with Diane Cirincione).

Jerry spoke with us in his modest office on a pier in Tiburon, overlooking San Francisco Bay.

**Gerald Jampolsky, M.D.**

**Jerry:** I would like to begin with a prayer from *A Course in Miracles.* We are here only to be truly helpful. We are here to represent he who sent us. We don't have to worry about what to say or what to do, because he who sent us will direct us. We are content to be wherever you wish, knowing you go there with us. And we will be healed as we let you teach us to heal. Help us step aside and be healed.

**Gay Lynn:** What have you learned in your life, in your relationships, about yourself and the birthing process?

**Jerry:** I see it as a process of allowing for my creativity. I came into this life feeling like I had some missing links. I was dyslexic. I was at the bottom of my class most of the time. Kids knew I could not read or write, but they thought I was a bully, not dyslexic. I think in high school I got a C- or a D+ average. In those days, you could get in the University of California-Berkeley with those grades, but you couldn't do that today. You had to take an English exam to get in and I flunked it, so I had to take a dumbbell English course my first semester, which I got a D- in. I remember the professor came up to me the last day and said, "Jampolsky, I don't know what you're going to do in life, but for God's sake, don't ever try to write a book!" I knew he was

> **I remember the professor came up to me the last day and said, "Jampolsky, I don't know what you're going to do in life, but for God's sake, don't ever try to write a book!"**

right. It was the last thing I would ever try to do. So most of my life I lived in a great deal of fear. I took a fear stance to life. I did what I was supposed to be doing out of fear. If I had any original thoughts, I would certainly keep them to myself because, as a kid, if I raised my hand to say something, it was the wrong answer! *[Laughter.]*

In medical school I did very well in anatomy. As a dyslexic, I can touch and learn something. When it came to looking at things through microscopes, I did very poorly because of my left and right confusion. In clinical medicine, I did very well. I was able to get the diagnosis correctly, but for the wrong reason. I knew it from intuition, from Spirit or whatever you want to call it, but not from the psychoanalytic standpoint.

So, I see the birthing process in terms of an evolution of my creativity—I never thought of myself as a very creative person or able to excel at anything. I spent most of my life hanging on by my fingernails and struggling through my anxiety. I did well. I went into practice. I did everything my parents told me to, which was: Work hard, make a lot of money, have nice material things. And that bought temporary happiness, but did not ensure happiness.

Then, in 1975, I came into *A Course in Miracles*. I was drowning myself in alcohol. I was scared to die and an atheist. When I first got the Course to look at from Judy Skutch-Woodson, a voice inside me said, "Physician, heal thyself. This is your way home." I guess that was the beginning for me, the opening for my conscious spirituality to emerge.

I knew there must be a different way of looking at the world or at myself, and the Course helped me *not* to give power to other people, like a professor telling me what I can or cannot do with my life. It helped me learn not to interpret people's behavior, only my own. Perhaps one of the most important things I learned about creativity was to burn up my evaluation slips of other people, and other people's evaluations of me.

Even before I was on a spiritual pathway, as a teacher at the University of California, I had some inner feelings that there was another way of practicing psychiatry than what I had been taught. So, I started to be an instructor, and later an Assistant Clinical Professor of Psychiatry and do some more creative things, and it wasn't received well. So, I decided I needed to be in a less rigid structure. I felt stifled. I left the academic scene. My soul was hungry, too. I felt my soul needed to expand. For me the opening of creativity—that creative birthing process in each of us— came when I learned to listen to the inner voice.

> **For me the opening of creativity—that creative birthing process in each of us—came when I learned to listen to the inner voice.**

At the time I was doing the Course, but I was still drinking very heavily, killing myself with alcohol. I was sitting in on rounds with an oncologist and this eight-year-old kid asked, "What's it like to die?" And the oncologist changed the subject. I became curious as to what kids talk about. They only really got to talk to the cleaning lady in the morning. I got some inner guidance that I should start gathering a small group of children who were facing life-threatening illness—that these kids likewise would be spiritual teachers, old souls in young bodies, teaching me and other people who would wish to be with them. We started the first center based on the principles in *A Course in Miracles.* Since we teach what we want to learn, we started with some of the *Course's* basic teachings:

- Creating inner peace by letting go of fear
- Forgiveness is the key to happiness
- The essence of our being is love

All these, and many more principles that open the heart and allow the soul to soar. And that's what started to happen to me. I began to realize my past experience wasn't going to tell me anything. I had to let go of my past experience, and come to *this* moment with empty hands. I am an amateur photographer. I used to have hundreds of photographs of people's empty hands just to remind me, "Come to the present moment with empty hands." Utilizing God's presence, love, and becoming a co-creator, becoming one with creation, is in the present moment.

I was having a lot of trouble with the Course. Because I was Jewish, its Christian language bothered me. It was difficult and I felt guilty doing it, and had mixed feelings about the whole thing. The word "Christ" I had to change to "higher consciousness." Because I was dyslexic, the thickness of the books really bothered me. And for many reasons, I developed a resistance to a lot of the stuff. At one time I didn't like the idea that Jesus was telling *me* what to do! *[Laughter.]* That seemed kind of stupid to me.

**David:** He was a good Jewish guy!

**Jerry:** Oh, he was a good Jewish guy, but he was still telling me what to do! I wanted to make up my own mind.

I would see people in my practice for 50 minutes and then 10 minutes later see another. And it would be one right after the other with no break. And the inner voice said, "You have to take 10 minutes each hour to meditate." I wasn't going to do that. *[Laughter.]* So I stopped doing the

*Course* for about a month and became depressed and agitated. Then I began to look at my rigidity and defensiveness and went back to the *Course* and started meditating 10 minutes each hour. I realized how much I was taking from one patient to another, that I wasn't really starting that hour clean. It helped with my creative process as a therapist. I was really listening from within.

It used to be that I was known as a good clinician because I had a really big gunny sack full of tricks. But I started putting the gunny sack aside and not using that any more, and started listening to the inner voice to tell me what I should think, say and do for someone. At times, I would take something out of the gunny sack because I was instructed to do that, but I wasn't doing that because I thought it best. So, part of creativity for me involved not making my intellect my god. I gave my power to God.

> **So, part of creativity for me involved not making my intellect my god. I gave my power to God.**

In terms of my resistance to the *Course,* I decided that I would make some white cards that I felt were just for me. What I did was put on them about 12 lessons that didn't have any religious terminology. That's where I was getting stuck. I thumbed through these white cards and kept going over the *Course* that way for a time. Once in a while someone would see me with these white cards and say, "What are they?" And I'd say, "Well, they're the synopsis for the nine-year-old me on the *Course.*" So, sometimes they would ask to borrow them and they would say, "My life has changed just going through these white cards." After a while, so many people's lives were changed, they told me to maybe publish a little booklet. So that is when I published *To Give Is to Receive, An 18-Day Course in Human Relationships*. It was my own therapy. I wasn't even thinking about other people, or even writing a book.

**David:** When did that come out?

**Jerry:** I self-published those in 1979. I don't have a good accounting on how many have been distributed, maybe 80,000, and we gave away at least that many to prisons and other places. We have given lots of these away. Then I began giving some seminars based on *A Course in Miracles*. I am a *very shy* person, and the last thing I wanted to do was get up and talk in front of people.

I was used to being a doctor and having everything written in advance, so I was always speaking from a script. And that stifled my creativity. In fact, that's what most professional papers are—scripts.

I was in England, giving a paper at a large conference, and I went to see Ena Twigg. Judith Skutch-Woodson had referred me to her. She died a few years ago, but she was one of the most famous psychics in the world. She didn't know anything about me and she said, "You just lectured and you're not too pleased with it." She said, "You can't really be creative and come from the heart when you already have something prepared. You have to listen so that you know what is supposed to come."

> **I'm dyslexic. I can't even remember the stuff I'm supposed to do! I think this is good advice for other people, but not for me!**

I said, "Well I'm not like Judy Skutch. You know, Judy can take one breath and talk without effort for the next 10 hours. She has this wonderful memory and she remembers everything that ever happened to her. I'm dyslexic. I can't even remember the stuff I'm supposed to do! I think this is good advice for other people, but not for me!"

She started to say some other crazy kinds of things. She was a nice lady, but these ideas were crazy. She said, "I see these centers for attitudinal healing all over the world." And then I knew she was crazy. *[Laughter.]*

She also said I would be in Israel in six months, which I had no plans to do. *Everything* she said turned out to be true, all these predictions. It reminds me that I don't think we are given information that is going to scare us.

**Gay Lynn:** Yes!

**Jerry:** I think we are given as much information as we can handle. But at the time, I didn't give it much attention. After six months I started to try to speak with just a few crib notes. Then the crib notes kept getting shorter, shorter and shorter. Then, six months later, I realized that I got up and talked for an hour without knowing what I was going to say. And to my amazement, people stood up and clapped at the end. I was shocked. I knew it wasn't me, it was something coming through me that really pulled all that stuff together. I could see how much I was getting in the way of my own creativity, my own fear of what I think I should say, and what people are going to think.

> **I could see how much I was getting in the way of my own creativity, my own fear of what I think I should say, and what people are going to think.**

Well, a lot of people began to share their healing stories.

People said, "You ought to collect them and put them in a book." Well, that scared me at first. I never thought the first one was a book. I had all these stories; it wasn't as if I had to go to the library and do all this hard research and work to do it. I prayed through it and had friends help me with the grammar and clean up the writing. My dyslexia helped me because I wanted cartoon-type graphics, big print instead of small type, and larger white spaces on the page. Some breathing room.

> **Simplicity is very difficult for a confused mind to understand.**

Simplicity is very difficult for a confused mind to understand. I believe Jesus taught by example, parables, creating personal examples so people can say "Aha!"

I think part of creativity is going inside to the very deepest place and allowing yourself to be vulnerable and to be shown your most inner core. There is a lot of healing in just sharing your story. Part of creativity is experiencing balance in your male and female energies. My wife, Dianne, is a good teacher to me. I think when we present together, people don't remember so much the content, although I'd like to think the content was helpful. I think six weeks later they remember the experience of love, and the quality of the relationship.

**Gay Lynn:** What experiences stand out in your mind?

**Jerry:** I have been very fortunate in that I have been by the bedside or at the hospital of many children at the time of death. Even if they were not supposed to die at that point, somehow I was there. Around 1979 I had this incredible dream. I was on a hillside and all the children that had died at different ages were there, and we were dancing around in a circle. And all of a sudden they started going into space and turning into light. It was a very beautiful experience for me. It reminded me that this is what the teaching is: There is only light. It was as if the dream were saying, "Hey, Jerry! You're on the right path." I believe these children are centers of light who are guardian angels for me

> **I believe these children are centers of light who are guardian angels for me when I pray and ask for guidance. They are there to help me on my way.**

when I pray and ask for guidance. They are there to help me on my way.

**David:** How have you stayed on your path, lecturing, writing, counseling, and nurturing and touching the lives of so many people for so many years?

**Jerry:** Part of it is a perseverance that I learned from my parents. Part is realizing we are only the vehicles for the message. So that's helped. There is a picture I would want used of me when I die. It shows me with this young boy, Tinman Walker, hugging me but you can't see *my* face. That's the way I want to be: a vehicle. I had no idea there would be over

> **There is a tremendous joining of people, coming together with hearts and minds, learning the hardest lesson there is: that there is another way of looking at life and death and finding joy in the process.**

100 Attitudinal Healing centers in 17 different countries. I would have been scared. It was never my idea to do that.

It happened; it wasn't my plan. My plan was to make peace with God in me. I didn't even have that plan; my plan was to just live each day. That's why we have grown—there wasn't a plan. There is a tremendous joining of people, coming together with hearts and minds, learning the hardest lesson there is: that there is another way of looking at life and death and finding joy in the process.

I think also that being creative is letting go of the manipulation. In my past life, I was a pretty powerful, manipulative type of guy. I used to have the biggest carrot and I could get people to do what I wanted them to do. Being powerful like that, you get to be successful as the world sees it—unsuccessful inside. Learning *not* to be manipulative entails being creative and allowing that energy to be. Let go of your controls, be a follower.

**Gay Lynn:** What does the Aesop's fable say to you?

**Jerry:** When I was a little kid, I used to believe there was a treasure at the end of the rainbow—and most of my life I have been trying to find that treasure. I wonder why no one ever told me that the treasure was within me!

I think the same thing is true for the story. Our ego keeps us separate, keeps us feeling empty, doesn't know about abundance, and only thinks about scarcity. And then we realize, *we* are the gift of God, *we* are abundance, *we* are in God's image. There is nothing we need to have, nothing we need to do, we just need to *be*. The provision of God is assured; the more we give the more we receive. We are the goose and the gold is within us all!

## Labor

You have come in
Like a wounded animal
That crawls into a log
To die.

Now
Do not think me
Unfeeling.
It's just that I have
Been through it
So many times
And seen it
So many times
And know
I'll see it again.

I will hold your hand.
But if you see me
Smiling just a little
While you're writhing and torn,
Please understand
That I know labor pains
When I see them—

And frankly, I can't wait
To see what is struggling
To be born.

PICTURE WINDOW
BY CAROL LYNN PEARSON

# 8

# Spiritual Symbols and Mystical Experiences

It was the night of the winter solstice, just before Christmas. We were in Kansas City, Missouri, with our son, Kirk. We walked out in the city of festive lights that sparkled amidst the cold darkness on this shortest day of the year. We huddled together in the frosty air as we reveled in the lights, aware of the expansive darkness of night that surrounded us. We connected with our ancestors who have commemorated for eons this double celebration, during which they danced and feasted to keep the cold and darkness at bay, and also rejoiced at the rebirth of the sun.

Our modern Christmas colors of red and green are actually ancient solstice colors. Red symbolizes the return of the blazing sun, and green represents the renewal of budding plants. After we took a walk in the lights surrounded by vast darkness, we arrived home to light a single candle in the warmth of our son's house. We paused to reflect on this ancient ritual of lighting a candle and embracing the darkness.

Why do we celebrate the birth of Jesus at a different time of year than he was probably born? We have long known that the journey of Mary and Joseph, in the birth story as told by Luke, took place in the spring of the year, not in the middle of winter. We also know that in the early days of the Christian churches, in an effort to blend the new religion with Roman customs, the two celebrations were lumped together to interest more Romans in including Jesus' birth in their midwinter solstice festivals. But celebrating Christmas in midwinter goes beyond the political decisions of church patriarchs in religious councils. Something mystical and magnificent is hidden in the middle of winter darkness, a time when people made the winter passage on the northern hemisphere of the planet.

> **Why do we celebrate the birth of Jesus at a different time of year than he was probably born? We have long known that the journey of Mary and Joseph, in the birth story as told by Luke, took place in the spring of the year, not in the middle of winter.**

We sat in the living room, enjoying the aroma of a few boughs we had cut from a pine tree outside. We listened quietly to the Christmas music from the CD player. We felt the comfort of darkness, and realized that so many of our Christmas songs celebrate darkness. Why is that? This is supposed to be a time of lights everywhere. After all, have we not contrasted light as good and darkness as bad; likewise white and black, day and night? Flee from darkness toward the light, we have been told.

We listened to the Christmas carols and heard them celebrate both light *and* darkness, day *and* night. The most famous and best-loved of all the songs, first written and sung for a Christmas Eve service in a little church in Germany, tenderly embraces the darkness: "Silent Night."

Silent night! Holy night!
All is calm, all is bright.
Round yon virgin, mother and child.
Holy infant, so tender and mild.
Sleep in heavenly peace.
Sleep in heavenly peace.

Why do we have Jesus born at night?

It came upon a midnight clear.

and

O Little Town of Bethlehem,
How still we see thee lie;
Above thy deep and dreamless sleep
The silent stars go by;
Yet in thy dark streets shineth
The everlasting light;
The hopes and fears of all the year
Are met in thee tonight.

The babe who was to become a bearer of good tidings comes forth not at midday, but at midnight. This gift, this messenger of truth, this healing practitioner, this way-shower of new life and love comes in the middle of darkness, born out of the darkness of his mother's womb, as we all are. Darkness was not a bad place, but where he grew, developed, was nourished and nurtured in the moist and fertile mother, Mary.

How could we have missed this rich reality in our dualism that constantly pitted light against darkness—with darkness something to be shunned?

Our awareness grew as we rolled back the prejudices we had formed about darkness as evil and foreboding on that winter solstice. When does Santa Claus come across the sky bearing gifts? How does he get into the house? Why does Santa need the now legendary Rudolph and his bright red nose to guide him? All the images here are of gifts coming to us in the middle of the night, in darkness.

> **The babe who was to become a bearer of good tidings comes forth not at midday, but at midnight. This gift, this messenger of truth, this healing practitioner, this way-shower of new life and love comes in the middle of darkness, born out of the darkness of his mother's womb, as we all are. Darkness was not a bad place, but where he grew, developed, was nourished and nurtured in the moist and fertile mother, Mary.**

Maybe there is a profound lesson for us here. The prototype for many of the traditions around the Virgin Mary duplicated closely the legends of Egypt's Isis, sometimes called the Black Madonna. Other observations of sacred darkness range from Biblical references to God being revealed from a cloud of darkness to the traditional black cover of the Holy Bible itself.

Our quiet contemplation experience on the solstice may have been part of the cycle of death and rebirth, a transition point of putting the past behind us and ushering in the future. David wrote about the mystical quality of night in the celebration of Christmas.

## O Gentle Darkness

I embrace you, Gentle Darkness.
You have been given bad press.
You have been run from in ignorance of your gifts.
You bring us Christmas, at the ebb of the year in
celebrating the longest nights of the year.
You bring us Santa Claus,
coming in the night down the dark chimney.
You bring us the wonder child in the manger
from the dark womb of Mary.
Oh, Holy Night—Silent Night,
I celebrate you.
Sacred Darkness, my darkness, creative womb,
You are the matrix of my new birth.
I embrace you, Gentle Darkness.

*David Williamson*

Our birth is
but an awakening,
the beginning of a
cycle of little births
and deaths that
span a lifetime.

# Thoughts from Gay Lynn:

## Birthing a New Life, with Walter Starcke

I sat in a cozy room with handmade furniture and a high cathedral ceiling. The room was appropriately called "Treetop," reflecting the view overlooking the patchwork of pasture lands and trees stretching across the beautiful Texas hill country. Severe drought caused the Guadalupe River to be lower than it had been in years. I remembered floating down that river with friends several years before on my first visit to the Guadalupe River Ranch. The ranch is owned and operated by my friend Walter Starcke, an author, producer and developer of this experiential learning center and resort which attracts thousands of people from all over the world for group meetings and personal retreats, including executive retreats for Fortune 500 Companies.

I slipped into a reverie, recounting my first visit to the ranch. I had sat by the stone fireplace in the plush country living room eight years before and listened to Walter's amazing stories about Joel Goldsmith, Tennessee Williams, Truman Capote, and many others in the New York theater scene. I laughed together with my new husband, David, whom I had married that same year. Having some time at the ranch away from our busy urban ministry was a treat. Walter asked me if I had ever seen the grotto with the Black

Madonna. I was not familiar with that name and accepted his invitation to visit the grotto.

It was a warm Texas summer and the grotto was a small cave-like structure with a round opening. As I approached it, I felt compelled to take my shoes off before entering the interior chamber. I sensed that I was about to enter a holy place and I needed to honor it by removing my shoes and planting my feet firmly on the earthen floor. Upon entering the grotto from the bright sunlight, it took a moment for my eyes to adjust to the candlelit interior. There before me stood the beautiful Black Madonna. I felt her live presence in the little womb of the earth. My abdomen softened, and I felt a sob begin to rise from within. In a few moments I surrendered to the feelings and big tears rolled down my cheeks as my body heaved with sighs of release and heavy breathing. There were no rational thoughts nor analysis accompanying the experience, only a tangible sense of connecting with my primal memory of belonging to an intricate web of life that I had somehow forgotten in my struggle to comprehend and master life. Now I stood alone in the presence of this powerful image of the Divine Feminine that was bold, energetic, and filled with immense compassion that completely permeated every layer of my being.

> **Now I stood alone in the presence of this powerful image of the Divine Feminine that was bold, energetic, and filled with immense compassion that completely permeated every layer of my being.**

I stayed in the candlelit radiance of the grotto for a long time, leisurely absorbing the nuances of this incredible spirit. Before departing I felt as though I wanted to leave something of myself in the grotto to seal my friendship with the Black Madonna. I was wearing a special ring with a radiating sun fashioned in gold that David had given me. I pressed the ring into the soft wax at the base of the Madonna and noticed in the same moment the identical pattern of the sun on her flowing gown. Right then she spoke to me, in my heart, and said, "I am with you always!" Again, tears filled my eyes as I felt overwhelmed by my connection with the Black Madonna and her great love.

My life has never been the same since that experience in the grotto. The woman who entered the grotto was not the same woman who came out! I began on a new path in that moment. Back at the cottage, I shared my experience with David. We talked about the impact and significance of my dramatic encounter with the Divine Feminine at the ranch.

That night I had the most profound dream experiences. The Black Madonna came to me and opened to me a greater dimension of my life. In the dream, as in the grotto, I experienced the feeling of being deeply loved. This was not a sweet or light kind of love, but a love that transcended lifetimes of pain, struggle, and emergence, connecting to my soul on a personal level. It was the powerful experience of a relationship that had always existed, yet for the first time I could fully acknowledge its resource of life energy and vitality. She held me in her arms and rocked me. At times her face appeared as my own mother's.

Simultaneously, I felt the rage, anger, power, and dominance of a patriarchal God that was controlling, domineering, unavailable. I was furious with God as I had come to know God at that point in time. The Divine Mother held me tightly and reassured me that she knew how I felt and would help me through the anger. Upon awakening, I was covered with sweat, my heart pounding.

In the morning I talked about the unusual dreams to many ministers and spiritual teachers who were gathered. I felt embarrassed as I described my anger toward God and the experience of this Black Madonna who held me so intimately in her arms. They listened with love, yet they had no explanation to help me make sense of this strange dream.

The Black Madonna, as a symbol of the Divine Feminine, carries titles such as Lady of Heaven, Womanly Tenderness, Sisterly Love, The Beautiful and the Beloved, Lady of Abundance, Mistress of Magic and the Great Enchantress. I knew that she was much more than some shrine or figure for me to worship on the outer level, but rather that she awakened something within me.

After we left the ranch, the Black Madonna continued to visit me in my dreams. Her messages were always direct, filled with a passion, helping me to see the bigger picture. I began to hear more people talk about her—such people as noted Jungian psychologist Marion Woodman. I read about the Black Madonna as Isis, the famous mother figure of ancient Egypt that many consider the forerunner of the Virgin Mary traditions in Christianity. I gave my full attention whenever I heard mention of the Black Madonna. I felt a tingle in my body, a stirring in my gut. The Black Madonna as a symbol, image, metaphor bore an important message for my life and— I sensed—for the world. She spoke to me in my heart, saying:

*I am the wisdom of the ages, asleep in the womb of your being.*

*I awaken in you the remembrance of all the mothers whose wombs were the channels of life.*

*I have been hidden away in the cave of your unconsciousness, in the dark places in the earth.*

*Always present yet not acknowledged, always available*
  *but unseen.*
*Now I am visiting your dreams, my energy stirring in*
  *your heart, my passion alive in you!*
*Let the message emerge in each person as it will.*
*Follow it, follow the mystery.*

The Black Madonna taught me enormous lessons about my own sexuality and erotic energy and how to express these powers in my life as new creations. I had given birth to physical children, and yet the Black Madonna was showing me how to also utilize my fertility, sexuality and spirituality to birth divine creations such as a master's degree, books, a new life ministry, a different way of parenting, a sharing and mutually respectful relationship with my partner. I began to accept my own body as the chalice of the Spirit, and I was impregnated by that Spirit. There was a sacredness within my being that was different. It was earthy and sensual and moist. It was not in my head; all my energy centers were vibrating with her energy. I later read that the Black Madonna represents all these aspects. She is the intersection of spirituality and sexuality. She is nature impregnated by Spirit, and the sacredness of matter.

On the journey I realized I am the modern Madonna, giving birth daily. Each of us is, men and women alike.

Walter Starcke, a successful Broadway producer and actor, left New York for a number of years after producing *I Am a Camera*, known later in its musical version as *Cabaret*. During that period when he was part of the New York scene, Walter recalls being invited to a dinner party in Gramercy Park for then-famous playwright, Sidney Kingsley.

The host was delaying dinner, waiting for the arrival of

**Walter Starcke**

Martha Graham, the diva of modern dance. Walter recalls, "Martha represented the Divine Feminine energy because she had liberated the pelvis in dance. Before that time all the classic dancers had frozen the pelvis, the womb, and Martha Graham liberated that, used it, and a lot of people thought that was awful and vulgar."

The party continued and after waiting a time for Martha Graham, the host suggested that everyone begin eating. Walter recalls, "As we were seated in the dining room, Martha walked in blind drunk!" He said he did not realize that Graham occasionally had this problem. It taught him an important lesson that liberated him: The larger the lip of the funnel,

> **In other words, says Walter, "The more creative the baby you're going to deliver, the greater the pressure on your humanity to deliver it."**

the greater the pressure on the spout. In other words, says Walter, "The more creative the baby you're going to deliver, the greater the pressure on your humanity to deliver it.

"Many people would love to be a famous dancer, write plays or books, be a movie star, or act on Broadway, but they don't want to pay the price of holding the creative tension in order to do it. There is always a price to pay, and sometimes it has to do with one's integrity. No one has perfect integrity all the time." Walter suggests, "The object is not to have perfect integrity; the object is to recognize that integrity and hold on to it as long as you can."

To hold on to his own integrity, at age 54 Walter left the stage, public speaking, the platform. For a man who had made his life career before audiences and in the public limelight, this required a tremendous "letting go." Friend and colleague

Fenwick Holmes, brother of Ernest Holmes, said to Walter before he retreated from the world 14 years ago, "I've seen them come and go, Walter, and they all eventually lose their integrity. You've got yours now. Hang on to it!"

Walter felt that to stay in that lifestyle, on center stage, he would eventually lose his integrity, so with grace and dignity he left. His new mission was to open himself to a more contemplative lifestyle. A short time later, Walter birthed his well-loved book called *The Double Thread,* a spiritual guidebook for truth seekers.

"Birth is a giving," says Walter, "and what you receive in life is through your giving. You can't give birth without some birth pains. They are a necessary part of the process. Use everything—but don't be used by anything. Every experience, good or bad, is here to make us conscious, good or bad, everything is here with information. What we need to do is ask in every situation, 'What's the information here? What am I learning out of this?'"

> **You can't give birth without some birth pains. They are a necessary part of the process. Use everything—but don't be used by anything. Every experience, good or bad, is here to make us conscious, good or bad, everything is here with information.**

Walter kept his integrity by letting one form of his life pass away. He makes an analogy with the physical body. "Eventually the body loses its integrity and must be put into the grave to then disintegrate into the earth. So in our life, when guidance comes that a metamorphosis is about to take place, our cooperation is needed for its fulfillment. When we resist, we often put ourselves in a position of clinging to what is outlived, and we lose our integrity or our ability to be entire and whole. We are no longer in our own honest self. We are in an impaired state of being. Many of us stay in this state and are afraid to die from the old relationship, life work, or whatever situation. Yet this is an important signal of our maturation and growth.

"These are not just outer steps in maturation," he says. "They are also inner rituals that are taking place in us all the time. The little deaths and rebirths happen again and again within one lifetime. When our guidance comes for us to move into the next stage of our spiritual evolution, we need to celebrate and mark, with a ritual, the next stage of our spiritual evolution. We need to gracefully celebrate the fruitfulness of what was, and move on."

Walter responded to several of our questions on the Divine Feminine and Masculine.

**Gay Lynn:** How do you access your feminine energy and balance that with your masculine energy?

**Walter:** It's what I call "double-think." We're consciously aware of our feminine energy, consciously aware of our masculine energy. It's not either/or. We can think of two things at once. I meditate in the morning and I make contact, which is like turning the music on. Then I go about my business. Although I am not aware of it, the music is playing all the time, like

> **I meditate in the morning and I make contact, which is like turning the music on. Then I go about my business. Although I am not aware of it, the music is playing all the time, like Muzak. You stop being aware of it, but if the Muzak stops, then you recognize, "Oh, the music stopped."**

Muzak. You stop being aware of it, but if the Muzak stops, then you recognize, "Oh, the music stopped."

So one can meditate in the morning, contact the feminine, intuitive, loving, feeling energy, and then, whether you're a man or woman, leave the meditation, go about your business and be sure that Muzak is playing. We get to the point where we can recognize when it has stopped. We are multi-dimensional beings with both a masculine and feminine. This is double-think, to hold both realities simultaneously and access the energy from both to guide and direct our lives. We can draw on one or the other when we may especially need that help.

**David:** Living from the intuitive nature as much as you do must be a little scary at times.

**Walter:** It's about living in free fall. We have to jump off the cliff. Once you're off the cliff, then you're living in a state of free fall. And free fall is living by grace. It's what we really learn to live by. There is nothing you can do physically or by trying to control the situation or the people involved. You may try to, or think you can, but the closest analogy is that you are in a state of free fall. If you start to panic, you'll start spinning and it can be a nightmare. But if you just stretch out and relax, you can have a great deal more control and direct your fall. And it is the opposite of what we think. It is the place of surrender, of letting go, of trusting. Some people are not willing to jump. But each of us at some time has to be willing to jump off the cliff or we're going to be finished.

**Gay Lynn:** Sounds like we need the complement of both Divine Masculine and Divine Feminine alive in us.

**Walter:** Masculine needs feminine. Neither one is complete without the complement of the other. And so we understand: Experience is wonderful, but if you don't have the knowledge of what you have experienced, it doesn't get fully integrated into the psyche. And knowledge is wonderful, but if you don't experience it in your life in some way, it is valueless. We need both knowledge and experience, the divine partnership in us all.

Oh, gentle
darkness,
I embrace you.
You are the
sacredness of Spirit,
impregnated
in me.

*Unity Village, Missouri*

# Rocco Errico's Balanced Heart

In his life journey, Rocco A. Errico, Ph.D., Th.D., acquired not one, but four doctoral degrees—in Letters from the College of Seminarians; in Philosophy and in Sacred Theology, both from the School of Christianity in Los Angeles; and in Divinity from St. Ephrem's Institute in Sweden. He studied intensively with the late George M. Lamsa, Th.D., world-renowned Assyrian Biblical scholar and translator of the *Holy Bible from the Ancient Aramaic Peshitta Text.*

Rocco's scholarly efforts resulted in a rich understanding of the Scriptures in the context of the culture, customs and language in which they were written. In the several books he authored, Rocco examines the Aramaic language Peshitta text and offers insight on first century Palestinian Semitic Aramaic-Hebrew culture. He explains the meanings of Aramaic words and customs in *The Message of Matthew;* explores the Lord's Prayer line by line in *Setting a Trap for God;* and clarifies misunderstood sayings and teachings of Jesus and his apostles in *Treasures from the Language of Jesus.* In *The Mysteries of Creation: The Genesis Story,* Dr. Errico presents his translation of the Genesis creation narrative and defines the role of humankind within the cosmos.

**Rocco Errico**

A brilliant conversationalist with a unique perspective, Dr. Rocco Errico lives in Santa Fe, New Mexico, where he directs the work of the Noohra Foundation.

**David:** Could you talk about darkness as a symbol of God?

**Rocco:** In the darkness of the womb, life is conceived. In the darkness of the soil, seeds germinate. In the darkness of the inner mind, ideas are born. Darkness is nature's time of rest, incubation, formation, rejuvenation; it's secret rendezvous, invisible powers, and unseen realities.

> **Darkness is nature's time of rest, incubation, formation, rejuvenation; it's secret rendezvous, invisible powers, and unseen realities.**

We also teach that light and white are only symbolic of God, but darkness and the color black are also representations of God. Darkness as a metaphor presents God as the inscrutable source, the unknowable, the unmanifest. According to the early Egyptian writers, the first principle is characterized as darkness. It is beyond all classified and rational conceptions. Darkness is mystery. Ancient sages symbolized darkness as an evil, horror or terror. Modern thinkers continue to depict darkness and the color of black as evil, sorrow, disaster, distress, ignorance, blindness, superstition and lack of light. This is based solely on a relative, one-sided point of view. And it is relative.

Black is symbolic of the feminine energy, because it is the creative energy. When I teach the Book of Genesis, the first chapter, I make the point that when God created the light, he didn't create the light to destroy the darkness. God created it to balance with darkness. That's why God said,

"Let there be light." And, "The light he called day and the darkness he called night." The Deity only brought darkness into balance with light. Darkness has its place.

**David:** "And the light came out of the darkness . . ."

**Rocco:** In Chinese philosophy, darkness is symbolic of the feminine, because it is hidden. The womb is hidden, the secrets of the earth are hidden all in darkness. The strongest creative forces come out of the darkness. And so darkness represents God—the hidden, powerful forces of God that cannot be seen.

> **The strongest creative forces come out of the darkness. And so darkness represents God—the hidden, powerful forces of God that cannot be seen.**

The light is that which is manifest. I am paraphrasing Emerson in a nutshell when he said, "Continual light, eternal sun creates a desert." Well, you can see the idea right away. Even light has to be balanced. Not only does darkness balance light, but light balances darkness. And the darkness must balance the light, because if we have continual light, nothing will grow. It will be destroyed, burned up.

The story of Genesis is about transcendent consciousness. Especially in the first chapter when consciousness awakens, the first thing it does is distinguish between darkness and light. It's not a division. When we read, "God separated the darkness from the light," we think *division*. But it's *differentiation*. And that's what an awakening, transcending consciousness in us does—it differentiates. The male and female are for balancing. We need the two forms together, light and dark, positive and negative, male and female. In Chinese philosophy, the female force is negative. Without the balance there would be no creation of any kind. The hidden powerful forces always come out of the darkness—not out of the light. That's why it is difficult to explain the *how*. It is difficult to explain the *how* because it's hidden. The real crux of how something works is hidden.

> **When we read, "God separated the darkness from the light," we think *division*. But it's *differentiation*. And that's what an awakening, transcending consciousness in us does— it differentiates.**

**David:** And we all came out of that because we came out of the darkness of the womb.

**Rocco:** That's right. Because life is a mystery. We are living in this mystery and we don't even *really* know *where we are!* People want to argue with me on that, but I have proven it to them over and over. When you try to identify where you are and take it to the farthest point, you don't know where you are, because we live in a universe filled with many galaxies, and we don't know the beginning or end of the universe. We do not know how to measure it. When all of a sudden you run out of galaxies and enter this darkness—well, what is there? Can we measure it? We can't. Not until some more things appear. So we don't know where we are.

**Gay Lynn:** So in a real sense we are still in the cosmic womb.

**Rocco:** Yes, we are still in the cosmic womb and we *never have left it.* And this cosmic womb is a mystery. I would say we are lost and we don't even know it! Just because we have named something, we feel we know where we are. So this is the idea in the Scripture.

In chapters two and three of Genesis, we have the story of the Garden of Eden with Adam and Eve. We read that the Lord God made the woman from one of the ribs of Adam. The term "rib" means "equality." The idea is that the man and the woman were equal, or, in other words, the energies were balanced.

The rib cage gives the body form and structure. So the female energy gives form to human life. It is in the womb that a human being takes shape. This is why the Biblical writer uses the rib as a symbol of equality and form for the female power.

**David:** What about the effect this story has had on women? In traditional teachings, it makes women appear responsible for the downfall of humankind.

**Rocco:** This is a Torah legend. We cannot take it literally. It is a fable that teaches a lesson. In Aramaic and Hebrew, the serpent uses the plural "you," meaning both of them were there, both of them were responsible. It wasn't the woman alone.

**David:** What point or lesson is the legend making?

**Rocco:** The majority of scholars know the old-fashioned interpretations of the Garden of Eden story are no longer correct, not tenable at all. Many people today still believe these five basic interpretations:

1. The fall of man—*not tenable;*
2. The origin of death—*not tenable;*
3. The origin of evil—*not tenable;*

4. Original sin—*absolutely nothing to do with original sin.*
   This is a church idea which sprang from Apocryphal and Apocalyptic literature, beginning with the third century B.C.E., and terminating at about 200 C.E. That's where those ideas came from, not the Bible itself.
5. The last interpretation is that sexual union was responsible for the fall of man—*not tenable.*

Today Jewish, Roman Catholic and Protestant scholars no longer consider these five interpretations as sound or proper explanations of the legend. Although scholars do not agree as to the correct interpretation, there are two explanations gaining widespread acceptance.

1. There is no such thing as total freedom.

Adam and Eve had only one commandment: They couldn't touch the tree of the knowledge of good and evil. But they couldn't keep that commandment. This means all life has parameters—no matter where we are, no matter how much freedom we have. There are boundaries even in our freedom. So it's saying, in living life, there are certain boundaries, and if we cross them, we pay a price. That's all. It is not some God judging us. Adam and Eve were exiled for their disobedience. No other punishment was given; they were simply exiled from Eden.

2. The tree was a deliberate set-up.

God wouldn't set up a tree and tell us not to touch it, because God knows it would be the first thing we would go for. So, the story says that the tree was *intentional.* We were meant to eat of the tree of knowledge of good and evil to give birth to civilization.

In other words, it is an existential explanation.

**David:** We weren't meant to stay in the garden.

**Rocco:** Yes! This story is a myth. Many myths serve as existential explanations of life as we now understand and know it. Another example from the story is that God makes clothes for Adam and Eve. Why do we have the idea of clothing in the fable? Clothing symbolizes the introduction of civilization. Ancient authors introduced civilization with the idea of clothes.

**David:** What about the curses in this story? God cursed the ground and declared that women had to be dependent on men.

**Rocco:** We often misread the verses, Genesis 3:14 and 17, which talk about the curses. God only cursed the serpent and the ground. God never cursed the man or the woman. The serpent represents a false notion or a lying thought. The cursing of the ground refers to the difficulty of working and tilling the earth for fruitage or produce. Again, these curses signify an existential explanation about certain things in life. The writer believes that plowing is extremely laborious because it is cursed. It is so difficult to make the earth yield all its goodness to us. A cursed serpent symbolizes negative thoughts that lead us into trouble.

The idea of women being dependent on men is the biblical writer's idea that he added to the story. Technically, Genesis 3:16 is called a scribal addition. It was added to explain why he believes women are to be dependent upon men. This was not a divine edict!

**Gay Lynn:** We have looked at Aesop's fable of the goose that laid the golden eggs. The farmer's greed causes him to kill the goose.

**Rocco:** Isn't that typical of us? We find something that can really produce and we drain it to the last drop. And then we end up losing it. To me, the preciousness of life is that life only lays one egg at a time. And you can only live one second at a time. That's all. You can't live five seconds ahead, three seconds ahead. You can only live in the moment that is occurring. Of course, when I start to think, "I'm going to live in the now," the *now* is already gone. Because you can't think it—thought can never live in the now. It is impossible. Only in *being* can we live in the now, and not when we're in the thinking mode.

> **Of course, when I start to think, "I'm going to live in the now," the now is already gone. Because you can't think it—thought can never live in the now. It is impossible. Only in *being* can we live in the now, and not when we're in the thinking mode.**

**Gay Lynn:** How do I practically apply this to my life? Being—that's the place where I am really challenged.

**Rocco:** The challenge is there because we are so much into our heads. If we weren't so far into our heads, then it wouldn't be so challenging, because we would be natural. We wouldn't be thinking about life, we would be living it. That doesn't mean I am doing away with thinking. Thought or thinking comes as an aftermath of living—not as a prelude. We have difficulty because we want to put the thinking first, before the actual happening. It's reversed. The happening always occurs first, then the thinking. We could end conflict by stopping the thinking, realizing the moment, living it fully. The moment I think about it, I'm already in the past. My being is always in the now. My head is always one second behind. Truth is not a doctrine *per se*. It is a balanced heart living in the now.

**David:** How do we learn to live the golden moments?

> **Truth is not a doctrine *per se*. It is a balanced heart living in the now.**

**Rocco:** By not trying to differentiate. The very fact that I call it a golden moment means I am analyzing it, I am making a comparison. Thinking causes me to compare. Whereas every single moment is golden and precious; some moments are more heightened than others. When I put it through my thinking process, I have made a comparison. I'm measuring everything I am experiencing. And the *measuring* is really what destroys it. Whereas every second has its own preciousness. And it is without comparison.

**Gay Lynn:** We are uncomfortable with our bodies. We have been told that sexuality is an evil. We are struggling with our own naturalness.

**Rocco:** A rabbi once said to me, "We are the only creatures who shudder at our own naturalness." In Hebrew, the words for "male" and "female" are the shapes of the actual

> **A rabbi once said to me, "We are the only creatures who shudder at our own naturalness."**

members of the body, the sexual members. The word used for "female" means a tunnel or a cave. And the "male" is the protrusion. In English we lose the Semitic imagery that describes the shape of the energy. The shape of the sexual member is the shape of the energy.

**Gay Lynn:** Many people that are near death describe seeing a tunnel. I find it interesting that at the portal of birth we come through a tunnel we call the birth canal, and at death we are received into a tunnel. The feminine energy is prominent at both our coming and going in birth and at death.

**Rocco:** The female energy is also death. Because it's thinning out, it's light, airy, fluffy, time to fly. That's why marijuana and drugs are female energies—because they string you out, and you're flying, you're not grounded to anything. The male energy is the grounding energy.

**Gay Lynn:** So perhaps part of our problem is being overly grounded.

**Rocco:** That's the problem—that's why we go for the drugs, because we have lost touch with the female energy within ourselves. So we take outward substitutes for the female energy in ourselves.

**Gay Lynn:** We were in Florida during spring break and noticed that many students spent a great deal of their time getting drunk. I realized that the classical cerebral, intellectual form of education does not leave room for the feminine energy. So these students staggered around with a beer in each hand, attempting to go into those thinning, fluffy, airy feelings.

**Rocco:** Well, you see our culture is over-maled! *[Laughter.]* It sounds funny, but it's true. That's why we go for the drugs and alcohol, because we have lost touch with the female energy within ourselves. Balancing these energies within us is the key: Compassion with assertiveness, rest with activity, joy with work. The secret is balance.

## This Birth Takes Place in Darkness

This birth takes place in darkness.
And not only is the Son of the heavenly Creator
born in this darkness—
but you too
are born there
as a child of the same heavenly Creator
and none other.
And the Creator
extends this same power
to you
out of the divine maternity bed
located in the Godhead
to eternally give birth.

MEDITATIONS WITH MEISTER ECKHART
BY *MATTHEW FOX*
FROM THE TEACHINGS OF MEISTER ECKHART

# 9

# Embracing Our Divine Mother

## Blessed Is the Fruit of Thy Womb

The Divine Feminine influenced the men who wrote the texts that became known as the Bible. Their inspired metaphors and images repeatedly presented God as a Mother giving birth. This fact may seem strange and even shocking to those who think they know the Bible, but have read right through these passages, and have not seen with their eyes.

Isaiah, poet-prophet, pictures God experiencing labor pains, groaning at the lack of concern for justice:

> *From the beginning I have been silent,*
> *I have kept quiet, held myself in check.*
> *I groan like a woman in labor,*
> *I suffocate, I stifle.*

Isaiah 21:3

Again, Isaiah sees images of the divine womb as God declares:

*Listen to me, Oh house of Jacob,*
*All the remnant of the house of Israel,*
*Who have been borne by me from your birth*
*carried from the womb*
*even to your old age I am he,*
*even when you turn gray I will carry you.*
*I have made, and I will bear;*
*I will carry and will save.*

Isaiah 46:3-4

*Rachem* in Hebrew means "womb," and is closely related to *rachum* or *racham,* usually translated as "compassion." In the nuance of ancient usage, this compassion implies a mothering, womb-like, love.

How have we overlooked or ignored in our synagogues and churches such obvious declarations?

*You forget the Rock who begot you, unmindful now of the God who gave you birth.*

Deuteronomy 32:18

The Christian apostle, Paul of Tarsus, a Greek Jew with a fine education in both Greek and Hebrew, was well aware of *rachem* and *rachum,* womb/compassion, when he quoted from the Greek poets, "In God we live and move and have our being" (Acts 17:28).

The womb is not overtly mentioned, but clearly Paul alludes to the womb experience. We live in the cosmic womb of the Holy Mother. We are nourished by her body, and everything we need is supplied. We are intimately connected and attuned to her.

Not only are we in the divine matrix, we are also called to deliver God into our everyday lives. Paul puts forth the image in Romans 8:22 (Jerusalem Bible): "From the beginning till now the entire creation, as we know, has been groaning in one act of giving birth: and not only creation, but all of us who possess the first fruits of the Spirit, we too groan inwardly as we wait for our bodies to be set free." We are in the birth process in our lives, ready and able to deliver, as men and women, the "first fruits of the Spirit." This refers to the deliverance of God's good into our daily lives and thereby into the world. We are all pregnant with the Divine! God can only do for us what we let God do through us.

> "From the beginning till now the entire creation, as we know, has been groaning in one act of giving birth: and not only creation, but all of us who possess the first fruits of the Spirit, we too groan inwardly as we wait for our bodies to be set free." We are in the birth process in our lives, ready and able to deliver, as men and women, the "first fruits of the Spirit." This refers to the deliverance of God's good into our daily lives and thereby into the world. We are all pregnant with the Divine!

## Birthing a New Humanity

To further our own understanding of how the Divine Masculine and Feminine unite in us, conceive, gestate a new creation, and deliver in nativity new life expressions of good, we undertook years of spiritual study—meditating, researching, interviewing many people, watching our dreams, going to lectures, reading the Bible, and combing through hundreds of bookstores and libraries across America.

We put special attention on meditating on the life of Jesus as the well-balanced person who honored both qualities of the masculine and feminine within himself and honored men and women in his life. In Aramaic, the language Jesus spoke, he most often used *abba* as the word for God. Abba was an intimate, endearing term of affection, like "papa" or "daddy," and it was the closest word to encompass "mother" that would have worked in Jesus' day. Now in our society, it is not only appropriate but necessary that we include the Motherhood along with the Fatherhood of God.

> **Jesus knew that he was bringing forth a new consciousness of humanity in that hour and described the contractions of that moment with the images of a woman in labor. "When a woman is in labor, she has pain, because her hour has come. But when her child is born, she no longer remembers the anguish because of the joy of having brought a human being into the world" (John 16:21 NRSV).**

In our meditations on Jesus, an image of great power and creativity was revealed to us. We behold in the rabbi from Galilee a whole person, expressing all of God. People sometimes fear and misunderstand the inner union of head and heart, masculine and feminine. The point is not to have men be more like women or women more like men. We are not talking about gender, but an *inner* spiritual balance of energies. We see Jesus as a whole person—uniting wisdom and love, strength and gentleness, practicality and vision, action and rest. He embodies the analytical and intuitive, the scholarly and mystical, the disciplined and free, the outer and inner.

He respects men and women fully and equally.

In the upper room at the Last Supper, Jesus empowered his helpers to be a creative, transformative force. We see this vessel of the upper room and the chalice of the Holy Supper as more than a place and ceremonial object, but as symbols of the womb. In the upper womb, a new humanity was being conceived, celebrated and delivered to the world.

Jesus knew that he was bringing forth a new consciousness of humanity in that hour and described the contractions of that moment with the images of a woman in labor. "When a woman is in labor, she has pain, because her hour has come. But when her child is born, she no longer remembers the anguish because of the joy of having brought a human being into the world" (John 16:21 NRSV).

In the last hours of his life, Jesus describes the womb experience. There, in the birthing chamber with the friends whom he loved and counted on the most, he shared the "birth pangs" of what he was about to face in the metamorphosis of his own death and resurrection, comparing himself to a woman in labor and repeating the key phrase, "the hour has come" (John 17:1).

Jesus gave each of us an image of how to experience our own deliverance. He was calmly centered in the truth of his being and moved with the contractions, breathing and birthing a new reality and life fulfillment for us all. After the resurrection, he commissioned all of us to the work of peace by saying to his disciples, "Peace be with you. As the Father has sent me, so I send you." When he had said this, he breathed on them and said to them, "Receive the Holy Spirit" (John 20:21-22 NRSV). Today, those expecting to give natural birth are taught that deep breathing is essential in that powerful act of delivering the new life expression. Jesus was aware of that when he breathed on his disciples.

Jesus invited us to join him in demonstrating the new humanity when he said, "Those who abide in me and I in them bear much fruit . . ." (John 15:5 RSV). As we read chapters 14, 15 and 16 in the Book of John, we hear the words of the Christ consciousness in the upper room of our soul, which now becomes our upper womb, inspiring us to bear this Christ consciousness and deliver it to the world.

And what is being delivered through us? We read in Galatians 5:22: "The fruit of the Spirit is love, joy, peace, patience, kindness, goodness, faithfulness, gentleness and self control." We maintain conscious contact with the divine, and we bring forth more of God as a labor of love.

"We must think about God as Mother as well as Father. We must think about and worship the Holy Mother and talk to the Holy Mother, and enter into that Holy Mother consciousness within us."

*—Charles Fillmore*
*January 27, 1929*

# Revelations of a Modern Mystic: Charles Fillmore

The Unity teachings have provided a firm foundation that has helped our faith to grow. We were greatly inspired and attracted to Unity because it was founded by husband and wife. Charles and Myrtle Fillmore launched a new spiritual movement. They modeled a blending of Feminine and Masculine leadership that radically differed from any other religious organization in the late 1800s.

Here was a new model: A wife and husband who were spiritual partners, equals, world teachers, and light-bearers to a society that had oppressed both men and women by stereotyping and treating them unequally. Their example encouraged us to see from the Christ perspective our common spirituality and humanity, and to overcome our *Paradise-Lost* state, where women have lost the feeling of power and men have lost the power of feeling.

> **Their example encouraged us to see from the Christ perspective our common spirituality and humanity, and to overcome our *Paradise-Lost* state, where women have lost the feeling of power and men have lost the power of feeling.**

**Charles and Myrtle Fillmore**

Myrtle and Charles Fillmore, in their approach to a balanced spirituality, addressed God as Mother and Father. We wanted to find something special in the Fillmores' writings that reflected this consciousness of balance. While at Unity School in Kansas City, Missouri, we took the opportunity to search the archives. We discovered a treasure—a manuscript of a Sunday message given by Charles Fillmore on the Holy Spirit. We shouted with joy as we read these words, imagining we were there when they were first delivered in 1929.

Imagine that cold Sunday morning in January 1929. Charles Fillmore, a white-haired man of 75, addressed his congregation at Unity Society of Practical Christianity, at 913 Tracy Street in Kansas City.

It was an era of unparalleled optimism for many people. The Unity School which Charles Fillmore had founded with his wife, Myrtle, had grown enormously during that time, practically more than at any other period, with its positive message of inspiration matching the pulse of the era. Most of us today don't remember what the decade of the 1920s was like. For the first time, America could see the dream of being free from poverty and toil. The "war to end all wars" had just been won. A magical new order would be built on the new science, and the prospect of prosperity filled American hearts. People could visualize millions of cars on the roads and skies dotted with airplanes. High-tension wires would carry power to every corner of the country, bringing electricity to thousands of labor-saving devices and machines. The wonder of radio connected the country. Skyscrapers, like the Empire State Building, were rising above cities with their concrete, stone and metal frames dwarfing once small towns and villages.

Little did anyone know that on Tuesday, October 29, 1929, the stock market would crash, and by the end of 1930 the jobless would number about six million. Economic depression would lead to another world war of unimaginable devastation. Yet, on that wintery morning in January, a visionary man of indomitable spirit shared some timeless words of wisdom for birthing our lives.

Imagine that you had heard on radio station WOG in Kansas City this lively man named Charles Fillmore address the congregation. Intrigued by his message and approach, you decide to attend the Sunday service. Since it's a rather cold Sunday, you warm up the 1929 Studebaker your family just paid $895 for, and which you drove to the theater the night before with friends to see the funny man of the times, Will Rogers, in his new talking picture.

You arrive a little early and are warmly welcomed. You take your place in the simple auditorium just east of downtown Kansas City, and Mr. Fillmore begins speaking on the the Holy Spirit. The program does not call it a sermon, but simply an address. He speaks in thoughtful, quiet eloquence, as much interested in science as in religion.

> *I will call your attention again to the subject of the lesson this morning. You remember, we are all here just as students, not to listen to a sermon, but an interpretation of a certain fundamental Principle in Christianity; i.e., the third, so-called "person" in the Trinity: the Father, the Son, and the Holy Spirit—the Holy Ghost, or the Spirit.*
>
> *This doctrine of the Trinity did not originate in Christianity, as popularly understood. It was introduced into Christianity by an eminent scholar of Carthage, and, like a great deal of our Christian doctrines, it has a pagan origin; but, nevertheless, it is good, and it was accepted by our Christian fathers because it was true.[1]*

---

1 The classic ancient "trinity" here referred to had been Father, Mother, Child.

*When we understand the real character of Holy Spirit, we will see that it has been and is being worshipped by men everywhere. The Holy Spirit is, let us say, the Divine Feminine of God. We know that God is Wisdom, God is Love. Love is the Holy Spirit, or the Divine Feminine, and that is the Holy Mother; and if you understand why the Holy Mother is so devoutly worshipped by certain religious people, you can see at once that they are seeking and inviting and bowing down to and using a certain Divine Principle, and that Principle can be used in a larger way and it can be better understood if we would get it closer to our consciousness.*

*The trouble with nearly all these grand principles of Being, so far as we are concerned, is the matter of separation. We don't study these principles because we think ourselves separate from them. We are not separate from them. The Holy Spirit is working in your mind, in your body, constantly, but only to the extent that you open your mind to it.*

*Now, according to this Bible, the early leaders of the children of Israel had a concept of God as exact Law, without love, without mercy, without compassion, but "an eye for an eye, and a tooth for a tooth" was the law. In other words, the law had to be carried out. There was no forgiveness, no grace of the Lord Jesus Christ. That came after. When that came, it brought to the consciousness of the whole human family this Holy Mother, or the loving side of God, and that was exemplified and demonstrated by the Lord Jesus Christ. It is the very foundation of the principle of forgiveness, and when we understand this it gives us a stronger hold upon atonement. We see this atonement is really the Spirit of God working through his love; and you know how forgiving and comforting and uplifting is the love of the mother in her great, loving heart. She sees only the good and overlooks all errors of her offspring. This is God as Holy Spirit, and God as Holy Spirit is doing her perfect work in us, just to the extent that we recognize it and allow it to do its perfect work.*

*When man understands this power of the Holy Spirit to dissolve the hard conditions of mind and body in himself, he has incorporated and is working with the Principle that will dissolve not only his hard heart, but it will dissolve the hard places, the congested nerve centers or the congested avenues through which the circulation of his body is functioning. This shows that there is an all-around application of these principles, and when we understand the power of love and give ourselves up to the loving compassion, the loving help and the comfort of the Holy Spirit, we come into an entirely new relation with God. That old Jehovah God loses his hold on us, yet we cannot disassociate ourselves from the law. We have to all come under the law, but the law can be enlightened. We can put the soft petal on this hard, exact law of the Truth coming always exactly as shown. We see a new way, we see a better way; that way is through the power of this Holy Love.*

*Now, Jesus Christ knew this law, and he applied it in the great redemptive work which he did. He reached the limit of the masculine consciousness and he said that he must go, but in his place would come this Holy Spirit, and that it was expedient that he go. If he didn't go in that personal way and dissolve himself in Holy Spirit, we could not get that Spirit within us. You could not get the personal Jesus*

*into your mind. You must get it through the dissolution, or
we might say, the entering of his mind, into universal
Principle where we would all have access to it. You never
have access to the mind of a personality, but if you would
imagine that personality is dissolving his personality, lift-
ing it up to a higher plane and broadcasting it so that
everybody would have access to it, you would have in a
measure, a concept of what Jesus Christ did when he
ascended into the heavens, when he broadcast the atoms,
or the electrons, rather, of his body. They became the
property of the whole race. He gave us his personal life,
and that was a great sacrifice. We are appropriating those
electrons, or those divine energies which he released. He
was the life of the world. He was also the light of the
world, the heat of the world, if you wish; but he could not
express himself on that plane until he became the Holy
Mother, until he was the mother of us all.*

*We are told that this Holy Spirit means "Comforter,"
but it is more than that. It apparently means "healer," it
means an advocate, it means "Comforter," it means a
sympathetic friend. It means everything that we can conceive as the helpful side of God, accessible to every one
of us, and we get it within ourselves; but so long as it is
something outside, so long as you think of it as an external entity, you don't get the result, and the whole crux of
the situation is that we must incorporate this Holy Spirit
into our spirit. We have, potentially, the Holy Spirit
within us. We couldn't live a minute without a certain
degree of Holy Spirit activity; but we can enlarge that.
We enlarge it to the point that we shall have All of the
Holy Spirit working in us and through us.*

*We are told in our [Bible] lesson this morning that we*

*are joint heirs with him; joint heirs with Jesus Christ. Just think of that. Joint heirs to what? Of all the Father has. We are joint heirs to the freedom of the Father, we are joint heirs to the substance of the Father, to the power, to all of those dominant qualities that make us dictators. But have we realized that we are joint heirs to the love of the Father? And that is not really the father quality, as we conceive it. It is a mother quality; so we must think about God as Mother as well as Father. We must think about and worship the Holy Mother and talk to the Holy Mother, and enter into the Holy Mother consciousness within us. We must become, in other words, meek and lowly, just like a little child crawling to the Mother and getting into her lap and resting on the breast of the Mother. Can we do that with a stern, unyielding, dictatorial old Jehovah? We have to leave that old concept and get right down into the forgiving love of the Mother.*

> **We must think about and worship the Holy Mother and talk to the Holy Mother, and enter into the Holy Mother consciousness within us. We must become, in other words, meek and lowly, just like a little child crawling to the Mother and getting into her lap and resting on the breast of the Mother.**

*Count everything as good that has entered into your life, when you once have entered into or made discovery of the Spirit of God, of the Divine Feminine. There is no other way to get into eternal life but to activate the Holy Spirit. And every time that you get a thought of the universality of life, of love, you are providing it more. You are pouring it upon yourself, and you can concentrate that upon an individual and give them more of the Divine Love through this inspiration or outpouring of your prayers; but you must do it in the name of the Holy Spirit of God. And there is one of the greatest secrets of our evolution—the outpouring of this locked-up energy and life in man, pouring out through and unifying it with the Holy Spirit. Jesus taught that to the disciples on the day of Pentecost. What did they have? Tongues of fire; they had new ability, new fire, the result of Holy Spirit principles.*

*This ability and this power, this upper room, is right here in every one of us. We don't have to go outside. You don't have to find an upper room in some building, but the upper story of your mind, your own body. It is your top head. Think about divine things. Think about the life of God; and all at once you can feel a contact between that upper room and love center down in your body. Then you begin to realize those locked-up elements. We are, every one of us, full of Divine Love, but we don't know how to express it, because we have not made contact with the Son of God, the Christ of God. But when you get the Christ of God, the I Am*

> **This ability and this power, this upper room, is right here in every one of us. We don't have to go outside. You don't have to find an upper room in some building, but the upper story of your mind, your own body. It is your top head. Think about divine things. Think about the life of God; and all at once you can feel a contact between that upper room and love center down in your body.**

*God, unified with the Holy Mother, the Divine family, and the love of God, you have contact, you have unified with the positive—and sometimes the negative—elements of the Universal Principle that will work out in your perfect salvation. And the beauty of it is that we can begin in the little things of life; in every little affair of your life, incorporate this Holy Spirit into that, whatever it may be. It may be you need more of Spirit, you need more of the love of God, the life of God and the energy of God. Release and let go of the life force. Give it expression, give it expansion. It is through this we live, move, and have our being, through this great universal element, God.*

*Let us, this morning, give thanks that we are entering into Holy Spirit activity; that the action of the Holy Spirit in us right now is poured out into the world, the world all about us, the new life-giving Principle. As we live, so may all live. As we make contact with Spirit, we give forth our light.*

Anyone listening to Mr. Fillmore on that winter morning in 1929 might not have realized that these ancient concepts would be considered so radical and unacceptable to the mainline churches that it would take another 60 years before his ideas would begin to find their way into print and serious discussions, initiated mostly by women scholars in seminaries across America. The modern mystic from Kansas City was usually far ahead of his time.

In 1929, Mr. Fillmore saw this denial of the inner Divine Feminine in ourselves and prophetically called for us to heal it first and foremost. We must fulfill this holy and wholesome task for our sake and the sake of our Earth. Let us be about our Father's and our Mother's business.

# A Bible That Uses "Father-Mother" God

We have offered a spectrum of voices speaking from widely varying backgrounds. The bible has been given special attention and emphasis because, though it is by no means the only spiritual source book for humanity, it is certainly a powerful influence for many who are reading this book. We have just heard from Charles Fillmore, speaking in the 1920s. He represents a metaphysical, New Thought perspective. Paul Smith speaks next as a Baptist pastor and Bible teacher. Lest you consider these voices, and others in our interviews, as offbeat and affected by some "New Age" views, we call your attention to *The New Testament and Psalms—An Inclusive Version,* published by Oxford University Press.

The text of this rendering of the Bible, which is based on the New Revised Standard Version, presents the prayer of Jesus, now known as "The Lord's Prayer," in inclusive language. This is not done for political correctness but, as we have found throughout *Golden Eggs,* the word "abba," used by Jesus for Father, is an endearing designation and would be the closest term he could use in his culture to include a "Father-Mother" concept of the Divine Presence. So the prayer begins, "Our Father-Mother in heaven . . ."

The distinguished panel of scholars who edited the Inclusive Version explain in their introduction:

> *The editors were committed to accelerating changes in English usage toward inclusiveness in a holistic sense. The result is another step in the continuing process of rendering Scripture in language that reflects our best understanding of the nature of God, of the humanity and divinity of Jesus Christ, and of the wholeness of human beings. . . .*

*Human beings are created in the image of God—both male and female. This means that every human being, a woman or a man, a boy or a girl, is equally precious to God and should be treated accordingly by every other person. Thus, the equal value of all people, both genders, every race, religion, and physical condition, is premised by these central biblical concerns.*

I call you
Mother because
you are, sweet,
gentle Spirit
of God!

*Kansas City, Missouri*

# Paul Smith:
# The Courage to Call God Mother

Just as with Mormon Carol Lynn Pearson, we discovered in our fortunate encounter with Southern Baptist Pastor Paul Smith that the golden eggs of Motherhood and Fatherhood of God could be found in some unlikely places. Truth is not limited to any one denomination, but will surface anywhere open and receptive souls will courageously embrace it.

Paul Smith has been a pastor at Broadway Baptist Church in the historical Westport section of Kansas City, Missouri. He has stood up for equality on many fronts. Most recently he put forth his Biblically based inclusion of the Motherhood of God and wrote the scholarly, readable and wonderful book, *Is It Okay to Call God "Mother"?* Then he started insisting not only on full female inclusion in all offices and functions of his local church, but also extending total inclusion for gays and lesbians. Many members of his church left, but Paul has the courage of his Christian love convictions, and has insisted that all people be treated equally. His book is banned in the network of Southern Baptist bookstores across the country. He laughs good-naturedly about the reactions and battles his ideas have created.

**Paul Smith**

**David:** What has your journey been like? Tell us of your convictions and how you have made your witness to your faith.

**Paul:** Yeah! How does a Southern Baptist from a hell-fire-and-brimstone God end up doing what I've done?

**David:** Yes.

**Paul:** Well, I've had a lover's quarrel with the church ever since I was a teenager. I grew up in the Southern Baptist church, and they kept saying, "Read the Bible. Read the New Testament." So I did. I read the New Testament, and I said my church doesn't smell like this. My church was real abusive. It was conservative. So I've considered myself a gadfly on the rump of the church, and I've always thought we could be more, we could do better. Jesus established a reform movement that was never to stop reforming itself. We settle for reforms of hundreds of years ago instead of doing what you all are doing today.

As a Baptist, I read the Bible, and then I would say, "Now, Lord, your Spirit is given to us to tell us how this fits for today. And that's going to be a different answer than it was a hundred years ago."

So, that's my basic mindset. Also I want to learn anything that God is doing anywhere in the world, regardless of the labels. I learned healing from the wild Pentecostals. I learned of the wonders of meditation from Unity. My spiritual father studied Emmett Fox and Unity

> **I call myself an evangelical, charismatic liberal! I think everybody needs Jesus.
> I pray in tongues and I call God "Mother."
> Something to offend everybody!**

writers. So, I've been pretty eclectic, although I take it in and I kind of "Baptist" it. I call myself an evangelical, charismatic liberal! I think everybody needs Jesus. I pray in tongues and I call God "Mother." Something to offend everybody!

**Gay Lynn:** When did you realize that God is Mother in our lives?

**Paul:** I suppose this journey started 15 years ago, when I decided to question the conservatives' teaching that men should be in charge and women should be doormats. I knew there was something wrong with that. I really listened to the Christian feminist theologians. I ended up totally redoing my theology. I publicly repented. As you know, repentance means to change our minds, and we have to be re-examining our beliefs constantly. We can't just hold onto the beliefs we had last year without examining and being open to new and better ideas.

> I ended up totally redoing my theology. I publicly repented. As you know, repentance means to change our minds, and we have to be re-examining our beliefs constantly. We can't just hold onto the beliefs we had last year without examining and being open to new and better ideas.

So, I looked at the major New Testament ethic of equality and partnership. Anything that's *one-up*—be it in government, politics, business, social relationships, education or church—is not the biblical ethic.

I set up a big night with my wife, prepared dinner, toasted her, and told her I wanted our marriage to be one of partnership and equality. She didn't have any idea what I was talking about. She never knew she wasn't free! It was in my mind, and I had to face myself, not her.

The real test of this equality business came when we decided to have three of our seven pastors at Broadway Baptist be women. That was really transforming, to begin to treat women in our church as professional, ministerial partners and equals. We have a triad of gender healing to accomplish. We have to see God's image in male and female. Then, I believe, we can begin to see the feminine face of God. If I can't see God's image in you, I sure can't call God "Mother." If you are weak and evil and seductive and dumb, then how can I apply that to God? I have to repent of my language about women. I have to stop referring to us as "pastors and our wives." It's a terrible disservice today to talk about "mankind," as if men were everything. It's discounting. We have to change the discounting old language of many of our hymns. What does it do to our psyche when we hear over and over that God is King, Lord, Father? Aldous Huxley says, "Sixty-eight thousand repetitions make one truth."

> **It's a terrible disservice today to talk about "mankind," as if men were everything. It's discounting. We have to change the discounting old language of many of our hymns. What does it do to our psyche when we hear over and over that God is King, Lord, Father? Aldous Huxley says, "Sixty-eight thousand repetitions make one truth."**

Then the third part of the triad is to wrestle with the feminine in men and the masculine in women, which leads us in part to the issue of homosexuality. We just lost 20 percent of our membership last year because I insisted our church be open to all, regardless of sexual orientation or the sex of their partner. We gained many more than we lost as we opened our doors to everyone seeking an authentic spiritual community. I think these are the frontiers of our faith today and in the days before us. I'm deeply concerned about the meeting of sexuality and spirituality; they are really close together, as you all know.

**Gay Lynn:** We also try to show that our sexuality and spirituality are related.

**David:** But we have a religious tradition that is built around a virgin mother and a celibate son of God as models for the ultimate good woman and man.

**Paul:** Exactly! Well said! Not only that, but in all the Christian icons and pictures, you see Mary touching Jesus, but you never see Mary and Joseph touching each other. What a terrible model for family life! I like James Nelson. He is the best Christian theologian, I think, who has wrestled with sexuality and spirituality.

**Gay Lynn:** What are his books?

**Paul:** *Body Theology* is one. And *Embodiment*. Those are two of his best books, in my opinion. My next book as a Christian pastor is going to be on homosexuality.

**David:** We see a lot of the disparagement of gays, women, abortion, feminism, even the so-called men's movement as actually being a war against the feminine. It's playing on old fears, prejudices, controls, power needs. And behind most of these efforts to preach against the feminine, to push school boards to slant education sharply toward so-called "family values," is a fear of the feminine in men. Men are afraid to see a feminine side to themselves. So they will not just make jokes, but will kill gays or women or abortion doctors out of this terror of that part of themselves.

**Paul:** The religious right is often extremely oppressive toward women and those they see as men who are like women.

**David:** You have birthed a church that seeks to practice the moral and spiritual example of Jesus, and you have paid a price for taking that stand. There certainly have been labor pains, I know, in this birthing.

**Paul:** Yes, birthing pains. What a treasured image. Isn't it interesting that, of all things, evangelical Christians are forever talking about being born again, and it's a feminine image? Giving birth. It's labor.

**Gay Lynn:** And we're midwives of the souls.

**Paul:** That's one of my favorite words for what we do! We see what God is doing in someone's life and we just help it be birthed. We are there to encourage, support, assist, and catch it when it comes out.

> Isn't it interesting that, of all things, evangelical Christians are forever talking about being born again, and it's a feminine image? Giving birth. It's labor.

**David:** It's spiritual obstetrics. And birth is messy and loud and chaotic.

**Paul:** But it's so exciting to be a part of one another! It's like being there when a baby is born. It's a miracle. And it is somewhat chaotic. We lost another 15 percent of our membership when we started treating men and women equally and having women pastors. They used that as an excuse to leave.

> **We lost another 15 percent of our membership when we started treating men and women equally and having women pastors. They used that as an excuse to leave.**

**David:** It was too much of being born again into a new consciousness and way of relating for them.

**Paul:** I think one of the most important tasks of leaders is to cause trouble.

**David:** I have shared that role of challenging people to re-evaluate, re-examine, research, renew, resource and reform. I have a passion for positive change and spiritual growth.

**Paul:** I have made a great commitment to risking just about everything to live this way of creative love as a person and a pastor. We have a great opportunity today to break through into a new consciousness and way of relating. And the basis for this contemporary birth is not really new. One of my friends, Jan Clanton, just finished a book called *Christ Sophia*. It presents the image of Jesus as Christ Sophia who modeled all the things that women did in that society—washing feet, serving, giving. Jesus was the personification of wisdom, which is a feminine image in the Hebrew Bible tradition.

**David:** You have a chapter in your book called "The War on Women." Is this a religious and cultural war of long-standing?

**Paul:** No question about it. If the citizens of one country treated the citizens of another country as servants, property, and constantly violated their rights and freedoms, what would that be called? If one country systematically abused, oppressed and raped the people of another country and then said that the image of God was only like the people of their own country, would this be considered a war on the other country?

**Gay Lynn:** Attacking strong and free-minded women is especially popular among the Christian right, but Jesus referred to himself as a person giving birth and he compared himself to a mother. He said we have to be born again and again. He treated all persons as equals.

**Paul:** Exactly. Jesus was always accepting people who were ordinarily not accepted in his society. He seems to have seen himself in both male and female roles. In Luke 13:34, he likens himself to a mother hen longing to gather her brood under her wings. I'm not suggesting Jesus was confused about his sexual identity. Just the opposite. Jesus was so secure in his identity as an expression of God that he could use a female image to convey his passionate caring and concern for all people's well-being.

**David:** So Jesus images himself as a mother and also as a woman in labor whose time has come to deliver a new and greater love to the world?

**Paul:** He certainly does this as we read in John 16:21, "When a woman is in labor, she has pain, because her hour has come. But when her child is born, she no longer remembers the anguish because of the joy of having brought a human being into the world."

To image the Christ as universal, as including both male and female as Jesus did, is difficult for many. For instance, some people have violent reactions to my picture of *Christa,* a sculpture of a female Jesus hanging on the cross. When Edwina Sandy's original *Christa* sculpture has been displayed, there have always been strong negative reactions on the part of some.

But there are also equally positive responses to this moving sculpture, such as an anonymous handwritten poem that was taped to a bulletin board at the Cathedral of St. John the Divine in New York while *Christa* was exhibited.

**Gay Lynn:** Could you share that with us?

**Paul:** Sure.

O God,
through the image of a woman
crucified on the cross
I understand at last.

For over half of my life
I have been ashamed
of the scars I bear.

These scars tell an ugly story,
a common story,
about a girl who is the victim
when a man acts out his fantasies.

In the warmth, peace, and sunlight of your presence
I was able to uncurl the tightly clenched fists.
For the first time
I felt your suffering presence with me
in that event.
I have known you as vulnerable baby,
as a brother, and as a father.
Now I know you as a woman.
You were there with me
as the violated girl
caught in helpless suffering.

The chains of shame and fear
no longer bind my heart and body.
A slow fire of compassion and forgiveness
is kindled.
My tears fall now
for man as well as woman.

You were not ashamed of your wounds.
You showed them to Thomas
as marks of your ordeal and death.
I will no longer hide these wounds of mine.
I will bear them gracefully.
They tell a resurrection story.

Anonymous

**Christa**

## Our Mother Love

God, are You Father? You
Are Love, our Mother, too.
Compassion has no form,
I know, and yet so warm
And mothering—close and real
God is, sometimes, I feel,
Drawn to a heart of being
Too vast, too close for seeing.
Our Mother, Love, you are
Not separate and far,
No farther step from me
Than my own charity.
I shall not ever trace
Your unseen secret face
Till I wish my own eyes
Have learned to look love-wise.
My looks of gentleness
Shelter the motherless;
My kind thoughts are bright wings
Of healing to hurt things.
In vain I shall look for
You save in my heart's core,
Not in the sky above,
But in my heart as love.

JAMES DILLET FREEMAN

# About the Authors

Gay Lynn Williamson, a psychotherapist and Unity teacher, has a master's degree in clinical and humanistic psychology. She is a graduate of Unity School of Christianity, Center for Humanistic Studies, where she received her master's degree, and Wayne State University, where she earned a Bachelor of Science in education. She speaks to conferences, corporations, hospitals, retreats, professional organizations, schools and churches across the country. She leads Women's Wisdom Weekends and has produced nationally aired radio and television spots for the Association of Unity Churches.

David Williamson, Doctor of Ministry, has been a Unity minister for over 35 years and also served as head of the Unity School for Ministerial and Religious Studies. He has a bachelor's degree in religion and philosophy, a master's in educational administration, and a doctorate in holistic health and spirituality from the prayer- and meditation-based Ecumenical Theological Seminary in Detroit, Michigan.

The Williamsons are husband and wife and coauthors of *Transformative Rituals: Celebrations for Personal Growth,* published by Health Communications, Inc. They served at Detroit Unity Temple, ministering to a congregation of some 6,000 people. The Williamsons recently completed a 120-city speaking tour where they appeared on numerous radio and TV shows. They are frequent contributors to *Unity Magazine* and have been featured in many magazines and newspapers. They now live in South Miami Beach and serve at Unity of Hollywood, Florida. They co-host a popular weekly radio program on South Florida's classical FM music station, WTMI. They can be reached at Unity of Hollywood, 2750 Van Buren St., Hollywood, FL 33020. Phone (954) 922-5521, fax (954) 922-2762, or visit on the World Wide Web at http://previewnet.com/unity.

# Permissions

We would like to acknowledge the following publishers and individuals for permission to reprint the following material.

Excerpt from *Discover The Power Within You* by Eric Butterworth, ©1968 by Eric Butterworth. Reprinted by permission of HarperCollins Publishers, Inc.

Excerpt from *The New Jerusalem Bible,* ©1985 by Darton, Longman & Todd, Ltd. and Doubleday, a division of Bantam Doubleday Dell Publishing Group Inc. Reprinted by permission.

From *The Prophet* by Kahlil Gibran. ©1923 by Kahlil Gibran and renewed 1951 by Administrators C T A of Kahlil Gibran Estate and Mary G. Gibran. Reprinted by permission of Alfred A. Knopf Inc.

Excerpt from *I Seem to Be a Verb,* Buckminster Fuller, Bantam Books, New York, 1970. Permission to use the quote by R. Buckminster Fuller has been granted by the Estate of R. Buckminster Fuller. ©1970 by R. Buckminster Fuller. For more information on the works of Buckminster Fuller contact: The Buckminster Fuller Institute, 2040 Alameda Padre Serra, #224, Santa Barbara, CA 93103, 805-962-0022, 805-962-4440 fax, BFI@aol.com.

# Bibliography

Aburdene, Patricia, and John Naisbitt. *Megatrends for Women.* New York: Villard Books, Random House, 1992.

Anderson, Sherry Ruth, and Patricia Hopkins. *The Feminine Face of God—The Unfolding of the Sacred in Women.* New York: Bantam Books, 1991.

Austen, Hallie Iglehart. *The Heart of the Goddess: Art, Myth and Meditations of the World's Sacred Feminine.* Berkeley, Calif.: Wingbow Press, 1990.

Begg, Ean. *The Cult of the Black Virgin.* New York: Penguin Books, 1985.

Christ, Carol P., and Judith Plaskow, ed. *Womenspirit Rising: A Feminist Reader in Religion.* San Francisco: HarperSan Francisco, 1979.

*A Course in Miracles.* Mill Valley, Calif.: Foundation for Inner Peace, 1975.

Eisler, Riane. *The Chalice and the Blade: Our History, Our Future.* New York: Harper & Row, 1987.

Estes, Clarissa Pinkola. *Women Who Run with the Wolves: Myths and Stories of the Wild Women Archetype.* New York: Ballantine Books, 1992.

Faludi, Susan. *Backlash: The Undeclared War Against American Women.* New York: Doubleday, 1991.

Fillmore, Myrtle. *Healing Letters.* Unity Village, Mo.: Unity Books.

Fischer, Kathleen. *Women at the Well: Feminist Perspectives on Spiritual Direction.* Mahwah, N. J.: Paulist Press, 1988.

Fox, Matthew. *Meditations with Meister Eckhart.* Santa Fe, N. M.: Bear & Company, Inc., 1983.

Gaines, Edwene. "The Goddess Meditation: A fantasy meditation using the Divine Mother's nurturing energy to assist in the forgiveness process." Mentone, Ala.: Prosperity Products. Audiotape.

Gerzon, Mark. *A Choice of Heroes: The Changing Face of American Manhood.* Boston: Houghton Miffin, 1982.

_____. *Coming Into Our Own: Understanding the Adult Metamorphosis.* New York: Delacorte Press, 1992.

Gibran, Kahlil. *The Prophet.* New York: Alfred A. Knopf, 1923.

Goldberg, Herb. *The Hazards of Being Male: Surviving the Myth of Masculine Privilege.* New York: Signet Books, 1976.

_____. *The New Male: From Self-Destruction to Self-Care.* New York: William Morrow and Co., 1979.

Groth-Marnal, Barbara. *A Pilgrimage to the Black Madonna.* Santa Barbara, Calif.: Red Rose Publications, 1990.

Gustafson, Fred. *The Black Madonna.* Boston: Sigo Press, 1990.

Hillman, James. *Anima: An Anatomy of a Personified Notion.* Dallas: Spring Publications, 1985.

Hubbard, Barbara Marx. *The Hunger of Eve: One Woman's Odyssey Toward the Future.* East Sound, Wash.: Island Pacific NW, 1989.

Johnson, Robert A. *Lying with the Heavenly Woman: Understanding and Integrating the Feminine Archetypes in Men's Lives.* San Francisco: HarperSan Francisco, 1994.

_____. *Transformation: Understanding the Three Levels of Masculine Consciousness.* San Francisco: HarperSan Francisco, 1991.

Keen, Sam. *Fire in the Belly: On Being a Man.* New York: Bantam Books, 1991.

Matthews, Caitlin. *Sophia, Goddess of Wisdom: The Divine Feminine from Black Goddess to World Soul.* New York: Aquarian/Thorsous, 1991.

Mollenkott, Virginia Ramey. *The Divine Feminine: The Biblical Imagery of God as Female.* New York: Crossroad, 1989.

*The New Testament: An Inclusive Version.* Oxford: Oxford University Press, 1995.

Nicholson, Shirley, ed. *The Goddess Re-Awakening: The Feminine Principle Today.* Wheaton, Ill.: The Theosophical Publishing House, 1989.

Olson, Ken. *Hey Man! Open Up and Live!* New York: Fawcett, 1978.

Pagels, Elaine. *Adam, Eve, and the Serpent.* New York: Random House, 1988.

_____. *The Gnostic Gospels.* New York: Random House, 1989.

Paxton, Tom. *Aesop's Fables: Retold in Verse by Tom Paxton.* New York: Morrow Junior Books, 1988.

Pearson, Carol Lynn. *Mother Wove the Morning—A One-Woman Play.* Placerville, Calif.: Gold Leaf Press, Text and video.

_____. *Picture Window: Women I Have Known and Been.* Placerville, Calif.: Gold Leaf Press, 1992.

Plaskow, Judith, and Carol P. Christ, ed. *Weaving the Visions: New Patterns in Feminist Spirituality.* San Francisco: HarperSan Francisco, 1989.

Proctor-Smith, Marjorie, and Janet R. Walton, ed. *Women at Worship: Interpretation of North American Diversity.* Westminster/John Knox Press, 1993.

Ray, Michael, and Allan Rinzler, ed. *The New Paradigm in Business: Emerging Strategies for Leadership and Organizational Change.* New York: The Putnam Publishing Group, 1993.

Redfield, James. *The Celestine Prophecy.* New York: Warner Books, 1994.

_____. *The Tenth Insight,* New York: Warner, 1996.

Redgrove, Peter. *The Black Goddess and the Unseen Real: Our Unconscious Senses and Their Uncommon Sense.* New York: Grove Press, 1987.

Reed, Donna. *Goddess Remembered, Burning Times, Full Circle.* "Women and Spirituality" series videotapes: Direct Cinema Limited, Los Angeles, Calif.

Rupp, Joyce. *The Star In My Heart: Experiencing Sophia.* Luramedia, San Diego, Calif.: Inner Wisdom, 1990.

Schneider-Aker, Katherine Christine. *God's Forgotten Daughter—A Modern Midrash: What If Jesus Had Been A Woman?* San Diego, Calif.: Luramedia, 1992.

Sjoo, Monica, and Barbara Mor. *The Great Cosmic Mother: Rediscovering the Religion of the Earth.* New York: Harper & Row, 1987.

Smith, Paul. *Is it Okay to Call God "Mother"?* Peabody, Mass.: Hendrickson Publishers, Inc., 1993.

Spong, John Shelby. *Born of a Woman: A Bishop Rethinks the Birth of Jesus.* San Francisco: HarperSan Francisco, 1992.

_____. *Living in Sin: A Bishop Rethinks Human Sexuality.* San Francisco: HarperSan Francisco, 1988.

_____. *Rescuing the Bible from Fundamentalism: A Bishop Rethinks the Meaning of Scripture.* San Francisco: HarperSan Francisco, 1991.

Starbird, Margaret. *The Woman with the Alabaster Jar: Mary Magdalene and the Holy Grail,* Santa Fe, N. M.: Bear & Co., 1993.